Bandits & Renegades:

Historical True Crime Stories

A CRIMES CANADA SPECIAL EDITION

~ Volume 14 ~

by Edward Butts

Bandits & Renegades:

Historical True Crime Stories

A CRIMES CANADA SPECIAL EDITION

~ Volume 14 ~

by Edward Butts

www.CrimesCanada.com

ISBN-13: 978-1533344045

ISBN-10: 1533344043

Copyright and Published (2016)

VP Publications an imprint of

RJ Parker Publishing, Inc.

Published in Canada

Copyrights

This is a work of nonfiction. No names have been changed, no characters invented, no events fabricated.

Kindle Unlimited

Enjoy these top rated true crime eBooks from VP Publications **FREE** as part of your Kindle Unlimited subscription. You can read it on your Kindle Fire, on a computer via Kindle Cloud Reader or on any smartphone with the free Kindle reading app.

OR

Click 'Buy' and own your copy.

View All Books by RJ Parker Publishing at the following Amazon Links:

Amazon Kindle - USA

Amazon Kindle - Canada

Amazon Kindle - UK

Amazon Kindle - Australia

View Crimes Canada Book at:

rjpp.ca/CC-CRIMES-CANADA-BOOKS

To the memory of the late, great newspaper,
the Guelph *Mercury*: 1867 – 2016

The author would like to thank Bill Kelly,
Robert Livesey, Library and Archives Canada,
the Public Archives of Ontario, the British
Columbia Archives, and as always the staff of
the Guelph Public Library.

Table of Contents

Introduction

Infamy, like fame, can be fickle and fleeting. Given the right circumstances and publicity, a criminal can become an iconic figure, even if others have committed more frequent and more heinous acts of lawlessness. Captain William Kidd committed a single – albeit spectacular – act of piracy, for which he was subsequently hanged. Nonetheless, he lives on in the lore of the sea as the ultimate swashbuckling rogue, the most feared pirate who ever wielded a cutlass. The American Wild West had gunslingers who killed more men than Billy the Kid actually did, yet he became the most notorious outlaw of them all. Such characters pass beyond the scrutiny of history, and into the realm of legend.

In some cases a crime becomes front page news, and the criminal achieves the sort of status usually given celebrities, perhaps even hailed as a Robin Hood type folk hero. Sometimes the story endures the test of time, as it happened with the likes of bank robber John Dillinger. But very often the notoriety melts away after the press coverage stops, and the once-famous criminal fades into obscurity.

The book presents the accounts of criminals who were Canadian, or were in some way connected to Canada. As with so many of those who walked history's dark side, the extent of their notoriety is as immeasurable as passing shadows. Patty Cannon was a nightmarish figure for black people in Maryland and Delaware, but her story is little-known today. Eddie Guerin was a career criminal who stunned the world with a sensational robbery, and then made international headlines with his story of an equally incredible escape. Guerin was a legend in his own time, but is now largely forgotten.

The *Clan-Na-Gael* attack on the Welland Canal was a big news event in 1900, especially since the Fenian invasion of Canada in 1866 was still within living memory. But today few people know about this act of terrorism. Henry Wagner's crime spree in early 20th century British Columbia brought him infamy almost equal to that of the train robber Bill Miner. But Miner is now a legendary figure in Canadian outlaw lore, and Wagner isn't.

As a member of Depression-era America's Barker Gang, Canadian-born gunman Alvin Karpis was certainly a high profile criminal. After his release from a long prison term, he again became a publicized figure thanks to biographical books on which he collaborated (separately) with authors Bill Trent and Robert Livesey. But since that time, even though American true crime buffs are familiar with Karpis's outlaw career, his name is not widely recognized in Canada.

From the time of Georges Lemay's masterminding of a major bank burglary in 1961, until his imprisonment in 1969, Lemay's name was often on the front pages of the newspapers. His notoriety was further coloured by the mysterious disappearance of his beautiful wife. However, he died in relative obscurity.

This book does not attempt in any way to glorify criminals, or excuse or condone their deeds. It simply tells their stories as impartially and factually as possible, given available documentation. The individuals presented in these chapters represent history's darker regions, and for that very reason we cannot afford to ignore them.

Patty Cannon: Devil Woman

"This woman is now between 60 and 70 years of age, and looks more like a man than a woman; but old as she is, she is believed to be as heedless and heartless as the most abandoned wretch that lives."

The subject of this passage from the April 17, 1829, edition of the Delaware *Gazette* was Martha "Patty" Cannon, who at the time was being held in jail on murder charges. She had for years been the leader of a criminal gang that operated with impunity in the states of Delaware and Maryland. She and her henchmen had been able to get away with their crimes for so long because most of their victims were black. It was only the discovery of the remains of a white victim that brought about her arrest. Much about this diabolical woman's early life is shrouded in mystery but, according to nineteenth century chroniclers who tried to piece together a biographical account, Patty Cannon was Canadian.

Patty Cannon was one of those larger-than-life historical figures whose deeds make them the stuff of legends, making it difficult to separate facts from tall tales. According to one yarn, Patty was a Gypsy (people now called Roma). "She was more or less robust, had a wealth of black hair, and her face, while showing the effects of her evil passions and dissipations, was more or less good to look upon. The Gypsy blood that was in her seemed to be dominant, for she coveted wealth with a passion that brooked no interference."

That description really says more about the bigotry of the time than it does about the historical Patty Cannon. A more credible account, published in New York in 1841, claims that Patty was the daughter of an English couple named Hanly. Patty's father was a hard-drinking wastrel who had been disowned by his family, so he and his wife immigrated to Montreal. Patty was born there, probably in the 1770s. The Hanly family moved to St. Jean, a town on the Richelieu River near the American border. It was a notorious hot spot for smuggling. Gangs operating on both sides of the international line either bribed, duped, or intimidated customs agents as they smuggled everything from rum and whiskey, to shoes, silk, and potash over the border. Patty's father joined one of the gangs engaged in smuggling contraband merchandise between Montreal and Plattsburg, New York, by way of Lake Champlain. If factual, this account of exposure to crime at an early age could explain Patty's lawlessness to at least some degree.

Sometime around the year 1800, Patty married a man named Jesse Cannon. One story says they met in St. Jean. In another, Patty left her home in Canada and went to Buffalo, New York, and it was there that Jesse found her working as a waitress in a tavern. Jesse took Patty to his farm in Sussex County, Delaware, near a village called Johnson's Corners (now Reliance). This location would prove to be strategic during Patty's outlaw years.

The Delmarva Peninsula is occupied by most of the state of Delaware, a portion of Maryland, and a small part of Virginia. The Cannon farm was just a hundred yards from the Delaware-Maryland state line. County boundaries had been laid out in such a way that a person crossing into Maryland from the Cannon property could walk into either of Caroline or Dorchester counties.

Delaware, Maryland, and Virginia were slave states. Although the Delmarva Peninsula had a few big estates that were worked by many slaves, most of the farmers were small landowners or tenants. Fathers and sons tilled the fields, assisted by indentured servants or the few slaves the family could afford to own. The peninsula was also home to a large number of free black people. They had either been born free, or had been released from slavery by their masters. They eked out a living on small, hardscrabble farms in the more remote parts of the peninsula, and were generally resented by the whites. The free blacks were extremely vulnerable to the danger of being kidnapped and sold into slavery.

Lucretia P. Cannon and her gang firing at the Slave Dealers.—Page 13.

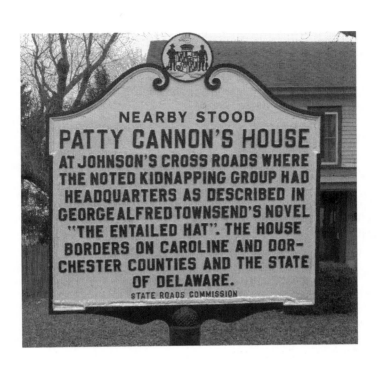

NEARBY STOOD
PATTY CANNON'S HOUSE
AT JOHNSON'S CROSS ROADS WHERE
THE NOTED KIDNAPPING GROUP HAD
HEADQUARTERS AS DESCRIBED IN
GEORGE ALFRED TOWNSEND'S NOVEL
"THE ENTAILED HAT". THE HOUSE
BORDERS ON CAROLINE AND DOR-
CHESTER COUNTIES AND THE STATE
OF DELAWARE.
STATE ROADS COMMISSION

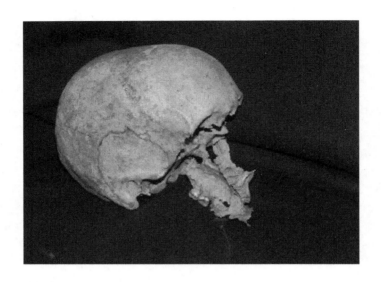

Skull believed to be Patty Cannon

It isn't known exactly when Patty Cannon first became involved in this nefarious business. For several years, she and Jesse lived on the Delaware farm. They raised two daughters, neither of whose names is known to posterity. One of the daughters married a man named Henry Brereton, a blacksmith who was a suspected "Negro kidnapper". It's on record that he was hanged for murder, though the details have been lost. The same daughter then married a man named Joe Johnson who ran a tavern in Dorchester County, almost within shouting distance of the Cannon farm.

Patty went to work in Johnson's tavern as a waitress. Contemporary accounts describe her as having thick, black hair and flashing dark eyes. She was a large, buxom woman who was stronger than most of the men who frequented the tavern. It was said that she could lift five bushels of wheat (300 pounds), and would take on any man in a wrestling match. Patty was always jovial and hearty with the customers, slapping them on the back and nudging them in the ribs as she served them beer and whiskey. But if any drunks became troublesome, Patty was the bouncer who threw them out the door.

More than boisterous drinking went on at Joe Johnson's tavern. Like Brereton, Johnson was suspected of being a "Negro kidnapper". He and his mother-in-law would form an unholy alliance, and events that occurred beyond the backwater of the Delmarva Peninsula would help make possible their reign of terror over the black population.

In 1808, the United States government passed a law forbidding the importation of slaves from Africa and the Caribbean. That drove up the financial value of American slaves. With American expansion into new territories in the South and West, and the opening up of fresh ground for the cultivation of cotton, tobacco, rice, and sugar, the demand for slaves tripled. A healthy young male field labourer who previously would have fetched $300 at auction was suddenly worth $1,000 or more.

Smugglers like the pirate Jean Lafitte of New Orleans profited handsomely by landing shiploads of contraband slaves under cover of night and clandestinely selling them to slave dealers. But smuggling slaves into the country was risky. The United States Navy patrolled coastal waters, on the lookout for "blackbirds" – illegal slave ships.

While smugglers tried to sneak unfortunate foreign captives into the United States, kidnappers turned avaricious eyes on the free black people who were already living in the country. Nowhere in the United States was a black person completely safe from the danger of abduction, but one of the most notorious places for "Negro kidnapping" was the Delmarva Peninsula. There, freeborn and emancipated black people actually outnumbered the slaves.

During the War of 1812, British troops captured and burned Washington D.C., and a British fleet bombarded Fort McHenry, which defended Baltimore, Maryland. The British offered freedom to any slaves who would run away from their masters and take up arms against the United States. Many slaves took the opportunity. American military leaders were even concerned that an army of runaway slaves, led by British officers, would capture the Delmarva Peninsula and use it as a staging point for a larger invasion.

That didn't happen. The British sailed away to their ill-fated attack on New Orleans. In the north, American attempts to conquer Canada had failed utterly. The war ended. Some of the slaves of the Delmarva Peninsula had escaped on British ships. For the black population that was left behind, whether free or slave, there was suspicion and hatred from their white neighbours and masters. It was the perfect setting for the criminal activities of what came to be known as the Patty Cannon Gang. Nobody in the white community cared if a free black person disappeared without a trace. For slave owners, the only concern was loss of property.

The men in Patty's gang were thugs from the streets of Baltimore and Philadelphia, and riffraff from the countryside. They roamed the peninsula, waylaying people on the roads and attacking isolated cabins, dragging off entire families. Patty herself would tackle a fleeing man, wrestle him to the ground, and tie him with rope she carried under her skirt.

To hold the prisoners, Patty and Joe turned the attic above the tavern into a 'dungeon". This windowless room was twelve feet square and constructed from heavy oak timbers. Captives were chained to iron ringbolts fastened to the walls. The only way in and out was through a trap door.

If the dungeon became too crowded, the kidnappers chained prisoners to trees in a woodlot behind Patty's house. A thick growth of pine, oak, and gum trees hid the captives from prying eyes. Two or three ruffians were always on guard to prevent escapes and warn away the curious. In bad weather, instead of using the woodlot, Patty would lock prisoners up in the loft of her own house. This wasn't out of concern for the captives' comfort and health, but because nobody would buy a sick slave.

The gang would kidnap any free black people unlucky enough to fall into their hands: men, women, children. Patty usually led the raids herself, but often her roaming henchmen brought their human plunder to her. Patty and Joe sold the prisoners to Southern slave dealers who paid cash and asked no questions. It didn't matter if a kidnapped individual had documents that proved he or she was legally free; the kidnappers and slave dealers would laugh at such papers and then toss them into the fireplace. A victim who persisted in claiming to be free would be whipped into silence and submission.

Many slave dealers took their captives across Chesapeake Bay and on to the nearby slave markets in Washington D.C. and Norfolk, Virginia. Others loaded their prisoners into ships for a voyage to Mobile, Alabama, or New Orleans. Whatever their destination, once the prisoners were placed on the auction block and sold, "freedom" was only a memory. They were now slaves, doomed to an existence of labour and brutality in the Deep South, with little hope of escape or rescue, or of ever seeing their families again.

Patty Cannon became an object of almost supernatural terror to the black people of the Delmarva Peninsula. No one knew when or where her riders would strike. Families on remote farms dreaded nightfall. Mothers frightened misbehaving children into obedience with the warning that Patty Cannon would get them. Travellers walking along country lanes would dive into the underbrush at the sound of approaching horses. People would wake up in the morning to find that a neighbouring family was missing a father, or mother, or child – or that the whole family had vanished in the night.

It was next to useless for the terrified people to complain to the law. The guardians of law and order were all white, and generations of a racist culture had made them impervious to any feeling of sympathy for blacks. The prevailing attitude was expressed by one individual who stated that if Patty Cannon couldn't catch all of the "free Negroes", she scared many into moving North, which he said was "just as good."

Nonetheless, free black people did have some rights under the law (unlike slaves, who had none at all), and some were courageous enough to go to a sheriff or magistrate when neighbours or family members disappeared. It was usually an exercise in futility. At the first sight of a constable approaching the tavern, Patty and Joe would just skip over a state or county line into a jurisdiction where the officer had no authority. If a constable managed to catch them unawares, they'd pay him off with a bribe.

Surprisingly for that time and place, the punishment for kidnapping a free black person was harsh. In Delaware, the law stated that a convicted kidnapper be tied face-first to a post (known as "hugging Old Susan") and given thirty-nine lashes on the back with a cat o'nine tails. He would then have his ears cropped (the lobes cut off), and be banished from the state for life.

The law was very unpopular with the white population, who thought it too severe. Juries, which were made up exclusively of white males, were therefore reluctant to convict defendants. Sheriffs and judges knew that if they tried to enforce the law, they stood little chance of re-election. Black people couldn't vote.

However, in spite of the overwhelming odds against them, there were occasions in which people captured by the Patty Cannon Gang were able to escape. In one instance, a man named Jesse Torrey, who had to have been either a free black or a white abolitionist, learned of a man, woman, and child who had been abducted. They'd been kept in the tavern attic dungeon for days before a slave dealer arrived to buy them. They were then taken to Washington. Torrey found the place where they were being held and somehow got an opportunity to speak to them.

The man said that he'd been in the woods hunting possums when the gang suddenly pounced on him. The woman, who had a baby in her arms, told Torrey that she had been asleep in her bed with her baby beside her, when three men burst into her cabin. She tried to fight, and bit off a piece of one assailant's cheek. But they tied a noose around her neck to choke off her cries for help and blindfolded her. The kidnappers dragged her out of her home but allowed her to take her baby.

Torrey went to a magistrate and had better luck than he probably would have had with officials in Delaware. He got an injunction prohibiting the removal of the three prisoners from Washington, thwarting the plans of the slave dealer to take them south. Then he went to Delaware and obtained documented proof of their free status. The Washington magistrate ordered their release.

On another occasion, a prisoner was the sole occupant of the loft in Patty Cannon's house. His hands were manacled, but his feet were unfettered, and he wasn't chained to the wall. It was February, and the man was scantily dressed and barefoot. No doubt, Patty thought that he wouldn't try to run in the cold weather. For once, she was careless.

The loft was over the kitchen, the busiest room in any rural house of that period. Sitting alone in the darkness, the prisoner would have heard all the usual noises: the fire in the stove being stoked, the cutting of food on a wooden table, the clank of pots and pans, the sound of voices. Then for a long time, he heard nothing.

Taking a chance, the prisoner lifted the cover of the trap door just enough to take a peek down below. He saw no one. The prisoner grasped the edge of the trap door frame with his manacled hands and dropped to the kitchen floor. Then he fled from the house, running barefoot across frozen ground.

By sheer luck the escapee avoided detection as he made his way to the home of a free black family. Those people hid him from Patty Cannon's hunting parties. They struck the irons from his wrists, treated his frost-bitten feet, and helped him slip out of the peninsula and reach Baltimore.

In spite of the occasional escape of a valuable prisoner, Patty Cannon and her confederates found the kidnapping business very lucrative. They were pulling in thousands of dollars, and the law either couldn't or wouldn't do anything to stop them. The criminal enterprise was working so well that the gang developed new methods of capturing "stock" to meet the demands of the slave dealers.

Joe Johnson acquired a schooner which he sailed to Baltimore. In the busy harbour, there were always men, both white and free black, to be found on the docks, looking for work. Johnson lured several black men aboard his ship with the promise of employment as deck hands or stevedores. When the unsuspecting victims went into the hold, Johnson and his accomplices slammed the hatch cover down and locked it. They sailed back to Delaware where Patty waited to take charge of the prisoners. Probably because of the transient nature of such workers, their disappearance aroused no suspicion. Johnson seems to have gotten away with this trick more than once.

Among Patty Cannon's many victims were runaway slaves. In every slave-holding state, men and women tried to escape bondage by fleeing from their masters and heading for the Free States of the North, or Canada. Maryland and Delaware were two of the slave states with the highest rates of escape attempts because of their geographic location.

Escape was a perilous undertaking for a slave. Angry masters went after them with dogs and professional "slave catchers". Mounted militiamen patrolled the roads, looking for any slave who didn't have a special pass that allowed him or her to be off the master's property. For a fugitive slave, almost every white person was a potential enemy, eager to claim a reward for capturing or informing on runaways.

A fleeing slave's only hope of reaching freedom was through the secret network of routes and hiding places that would become known as the Underground Railroad. Throughout this system were "safe houses" kept by free blacks and white abolitionists where fugitive slaves could find food and a place to rest. Quakers, whose religious beliefs held slavery as immoral, were prominent among the whites who took the risk of aiding runaway slaves. There were many Quaker households on the Delmarva Peninsula.

Like the sheriffs and patrollers whose job it was to hunt down runaway slaves, Patty Cannon knew the fugitives were getting help, but she didn't know from whom. For her sinister purposes, all Patty needed to know was that desperate runaways would seek help from anyone they thought they could trust, and who better to lure them into a trap than one of their own kind!

Patty owned a slave named Cyrus James whom she had either bought or stolen when he was just a boy. He would go down on record as a member of the Patty Cannon gang, but the question would always remain as to whether he was a willing participant in their crimes. He might have acted in expectation of reward, or he might have been a reluctant slave who did as he was told out of fear of punishment.

Besides labouring on the Cannon farm, Cyrus was used as a decoy. Whenever a master discovered that a slave had "run off", he would quickly alert the surrounding communities by word of mouth and with hastily printed handbills that were nailed to public bulletin boards and trees along roads. The information would also be carried in the local press.

Whenever Patty got the word that there had been an escape in her vicinity, she would send Cyrus into the woods on the chance that he might intercept the runaway. If Cyrus did come upon the fugitive (or fugitives), he would claim to be a free man who worked for a Quaker family that kept a safe house for runaway slaves. Trusting in a black man who offered help, the unsuspecting fugitive would follow Cyrus – right into the clutches of the Cannon gang.

A reward was always offered for the capture of an escaped slave, but it was usually only a fraction of the slave's market value. Patty Cannon wasn't one to settle for a $50 or $100 reward from a grateful master when she could get several times that amount by selling the runaway to an unscrupulous slave dealer. The slave, whose quest for freedom had been so brief, would end up on a plantation hundreds of miles away in a Deep South state, such as Mississippi or Louisiana, where it was unlikely the original master would ever be able to trace his "property".

After years of kidnapping free blacks and waylaying runaways, the Cannon gang expanded into abducting slaves who were not runaways. This might have been because the gang had been getting away with its crimes for so long that Patty and Joe became bolder. More likely, they were finding it harder to catch prey. Cannon gang raids had made an impact on the free black population of the Delmarva Peninsula; so many had been kidnapped or had moved away out of fear. Those who remained found ways to warn each other of the gang's movements and hide from the night riders. Moreover, word spread among the slave population of the treacherous slave who betrayed runaways into the hands of the devil woman.

Stealing slaves wasn't at all the same as kidnapping free black people. It was much more dangerous because it angered whites. The local sheriff might not be very concerned if a free black man reported that his son had gone missing, but he would be quick to organize a hue and cry if a master reported a missing slave. And if it turned out that the slave had been stolen, the consequences could be harsh for the thief. Conviction for slave-stealing carried a ten-year prison sentence. It could also mean death at the hands of a lynch mob.

Patty Cannon's abducted slaves went the same route as the kidnapped free blacks. They were imprisoned in the tavern dungeon and then sold to slave dealers who transported them south. Should Patty be caught in possession of a stolen slave, she had an ace she could play to protect herself from prosecution. She would claim that the slave was a runaway she had caught and intended to return to the rightful owner. The slave's protests that he or she had been abducted would have fallen on deaf ears; a white person's word was always taken over that of a black person – especially a slave.

Jesse Cannon's involvement in the gang is uncertain. According to some accounts, he taught Patty the tricks of the trade and participated in kidnapping raids. In 1816, so one story goes, Jesse was even arrested, convicted, and flogged. Only the protests of his neighbours prevented him from having his ears cropped. In other versions, Jesse deplored Patty's criminal ways.

Jesse died in 1826 under mysterious circumstances. Family and friends thought that his health had begun to fail a few years earlier when he realized his wife's true nature and his conscience began to eat at him. They said he died from grief. Sometime later, in her jail cell, Patty claimed that she had slowly poisoned Jesse with arsenic because he objected to her activities. It's possible that Jesse did, in fact, approve of the kidnapping and even engaged in it, but balked when Patty's crimes included murder.

Patty used some of her ill-got gains to buy land, increasing the size of the Cannons' Delaware property. She rented fields out to farmers. One day in April 1829, a farmer was ploughing one of those fields. He came to a depressed spot that was usually swampy but was now dry. As the farmer urged his horse forward, the ground beneath its feet suddenly caved in.

Thinking he might have stumbled upon the secret burial site of something valuable, the farmer fetched a shovel and began to dig. He uncovered a wooden chest, painted blue. When the excited farmer opened the chest, he found not a stash of money or silverware, but human bones and the mouldering remains of clothing.

The farmer reported his discovery to Joseph Neal, the Sheriff's Deputy for Sussex County. Neal went to the site of the mysterious grave, which by now had attracted a small crowd of the morbidly curious. Amazingly enough, word of the grim find hadn't reached Patty Cannon, who was in the tavern on the Maryland side of the state line, just a few hundred yards away.

Neal could tell from the skull and the clothing that the remains in the chest were those of a white man. Because the grave was on land owned by Patty Cannon, who had long been suspected of unlawful activities, Neal thought that it would be prudent for him to gather more information before confronting her. He ordered Cyrus James to be brought to him. Slaves weren't allowed to testify in court, but that didn't mean a sheriff's deputy couldn't interrogate one, especially when the apparent victim of a crime was white.

Cyrus spilled out the whole story. About ten years earlier, a Georgia slave dealer named Bell came to the Cannon farm and was hospitably offered a good supper and a bed for the night. He very unwisely showed Patty, Joe, and Ebenezer Johnson (Joe's brother) $15,000 in gold that he was carrying for the purchase of slaves. While Bell was eating his supper, he was shot through the head. Cyrus said that he was present when Bell's body was stuffed into the blue chest and buried in the field. (Quite likely, Cyrus had been made to dig the grave). He claimed to know of other bodies.

Neal and other local residents remembered that a slave dealer named Bell had visited the area years earlier and had then moved on without notice. That in itself wasn't unusual, and Bell might have been completely forgotten had he not left behind a horse – which Patty Cannon claimed. The blue box looked just like people recalled seeing in the Cannon house.

Joe Johnson hadn't been seen in the vicinity since the previous January, when he'd been warned that a magistrate in Philadelphia had issued a warrant for his arrest on a kidnapping charge. Rather than wait while authorities went through the legal channels to have him extradited to Pennsylvania, Joe had lit out for Alabama. Now Deputy Neal faced a similar problem with Patty Cannon. He didn't have the authority to cross the state line and arrest her in Maryland, and he couldn't take the risk of waiting for her to return to her home. If she learned that Bell's grave had been found, as she almost certainly would before the day was out, she, too, would flee.

Neal conferred with Sheriff's Deputy Jacob Wilson of Dorchester County. Neal was a Delaware officer who couldn't arrest Patty while she was in Maryland. Wilson was a Maryland officer who couldn't arrest Patty for an alleged crime committed in Delaware. The two officers came up with a plan.

Wilson entered the tavern, as though he had just stopped in for a drink, and engaged Patty in conversation. Always happy to gossip with the customers, Patty suspected nothing when Wilson said he had to be going, and invited Patty to walk a little way with him and continue their discussion. Patty was so absorbed in their talk, that she paid no attention to where they were going. As soon as they stepped over the state line, Neal appeared from a place of concealment and arrested her.

Patty was taken to nearby Seaford, where Justice of the Peace Dr. John Gibbon formally charged her with Bell's murder and committed her for trial. Then she was taken to Georgetown, the Sussex County seat, and locked in the jail. That night, as the town crier walked his rounds and called the hours, he announced, "Patty Cannon taken!"

For the first time, there was an investigation into the activities of the Patty Cannon Gang. Officers inspected the tavern and found the attic dungeon with the ring bolts in the walls. There were old bloodstains on the walls and floor. Cyrus James led Neal to the graves of three more people – all black children.

Cyrus said that one was an infant girl who'd been murdered in 1822. The baby's mother was one of Patty's slaves, and Patty had thought that the father was a member of her own family. Another, also murdered in 1822, was a young boy who had been injured and was a poor prospect for sale. Cyrus claimed he had seen Patty carry the boy out to the field at night and return without him. The third, murdered in 1824, was a seven-year-old boy whom Patty had kidnapped and then decided was "bad property", meaning that his free status might cause her problems if she tried to sell him. Rather than leave the boy alive as a potential witness, Cyrus said, Patty had bashed his head in with a block of wood. The skull showed evidence of such a blow. Cyrus also claimed that Bell wasn't the only slave dealer with money in his pockets that Patty's gang had murdered, but no other graves were found.

News of the murdered black children disgusted even white slave owners. But it was the murder of Bell that caused the greatest outrage. The killing of a white in a home in which he was a guest was treachery of the worst sort. Sitting in her cell, Patty Cannon knew that she was doomed. But she would not die on the gallows.

In the weeks following her arrest, Patty confessed to many crimes. She claimed to have poisoned her husband. Then, on May 11, 1829, the jailer found Patty dead in her cell. She had committed suicide with poison. That, at least, was what the official report said.

By the standards of the time, Patty Cannon was an elderly woman when she died. It could be that she passed away from age or illness. Nineteenth century jails were notoriously unhealthy places: cold, filthy, and vermin infested. While it's entirely possible that Patty had poison smuggled in to her, it could also be that her evil legend demanded a more melodramatic end than natural causes, and the suicide-by-poison story fit the bill.

Patty Cannon's body was buried in the jail yard, which was customary with criminals who had been executed or died while incarcerated. Sometime around the turn of the twentieth century, the remains in the jail yard were exhumed and relocated to an unmarked grave in the Potters Field of a nearby cemetery. However, the local deputy sheriff decided to keep Patty Cannon's skull as a souvenir. The skull passed through several hands until 1961, when it was put on loan to the public library of Dover, Delaware. In Patty Cannon's time, Dover had a large Quaker population and was a place of refuge for runaway slaves. It was the site of one of the Cannon gang's last raids.

Patty Cannon has appeared as a villain in American historical plays and novels, most notably George Alfred Townsend's *The Entailed Hat* (1884) and James McBride's *Song Yet Sung* (2008). She is still a figure of fear in the folklore of the Delmarva Peninsula, and the devil-woman in stories told around campfires at night. As for Patty being Canadian-born, if that part of her story is in fact true, the greatest irony is that the country that was seen as the "Promised Land" by fleeing slaves also produced the devil woman who preyed on them.

Eddie Guerin: The Man From Devil's Island

On November 25, 1878, the Marquis of Lorne arrived in Halifax with his wife Princess Louise, daughter of Queen Victoria, to take office as the new governor general of Canada. A vast, cheering crowd was at the harbour to greet the vice-regal party. Amidst bunting, a brass band, and military salutes, Prime Minister Sir John A. Macdonald welcomed Lord Lorne and the princess to Canada on a red-carpeted landing stage.

Behind a rope barrier guarded by police and soldiers, the jubilant throng pushed and shoved as they listened to the speeches. Most of the people there had bought tickets so they could witness a great moment in history. They were dressed in their very best. It was an occasion that called for women to be adorned in their finest jewellery and men to sport their gold and silver pocket watches.

The great event had drawn people from all over the Maritime Provinces. It wasn't every day one had the opportunity to see a real marquis and a princess. But the spectacle had also attracted seven people from Chicago: five men, a seventeen-year-old boy, and a woman. They were there on business as they stealthily moved through the jostling crowd.

A special train carried the celebrated couple and their entourage on to Montreal, where the scene was repeated. Cheering crowds greeted the governor general and his royal wife. The visitors from Chicago were there, drifting through the mass of people, taking care not to attract attention to themselves as they did their work.

The train rolled on to Ottawa, where on December 3, another crowd was on hand to welcome the marquis and the princess. Again the visitors from Chicago were present, as though they couldn't get enough of the pomp and ceremony that took place all along the train's route.

A few days after the governor general's arrival in the capital, an Ottawa police detective named Banning was investigating reports that a gang of pickpockets had been working the cheering crowd. There had, in fact, been news of such criminal activity all along the new governor general's route. In Halifax, Montreal, and now Ottawa, as well as at whistle stops in between those cities, spectators in the crowds had had their pockets picked and their watches and jewellery filched. Clearly, some opportunistic and skilled thieves had been taking advantage of the celebrations to ply their trade.

Meanwhile, the box office of the Ottawa Opera House was robbed. The method of the crime was one often used by crooks in big American cities, but one which victims in a small Canadian city like Ottawa, would not be familiar. Two men engaged the manager in an argument about ticket prices. While he was distracted, someone else slipped in and cleaned out the cash drawers.

On December 6, Detective Banning received a tip that the culprits he was looking for were staying at the Peerless Hotel. There were seven of them; six males and a female – all American. They were preparing to leave town that night on a ten o'clock train.

Banning quickly organized a raid. He took a squad of constables to the hotel and placed guards at all the doors. He went inside and found the suspects in a small parlour off the dining room, enjoying drinks and cigars. They seemed to realize at once that Banning was a cop, and they bolted for the exits. But with every door covered, there was no escape.

Banning placed them all under arrest and took them to the Ottawa jail. They gave their names as Mary Stanley, W.D. Smith,

William Miller, J.P. Stanley, A.B. Donaldson, John P. St. Clair, and William Petrie. They all pleaded innocence and expressed great indignation over being arrested. Mary Stanley, who was "crying quarts", as one reporter put it, claimed that J.P. Stanley was her brother. However, the Ottawa *Citizen* reported that when the police first saw them in the hotel, "she was being very affectionately kissed by her brother, something unnatural for sisters and brothers to be guilty of [even] in these degenerate days."

The suspects had more than $3,800 in Canadian and American cash on them, a pretty substantial amount of money for that time. No stolen property was found in their baggage or their hotel rooms, but a search of the parlour in which they'd been arrested turned up a gold watch hidden under a sofa cushion. The watch, which was inscribed, belonged to a local militia officer who'd reported it stolen. Undoubtedly one of the thieves had stuffed it out of sight during Banning's raid. But with Ottawa crowded with visitors because of the special occasion, and hundreds of people checking in and out of the hotels, it would be impossible to prove that one of the Americans had pilfered it.

In those days almost everything going in and out of a community went by rail, so Detective Banning's investigation took him to the Ottawa train station. He learned from the manager of the Canadian Express office that a man named P. Guerin had sent a large package to a Miss M. Connell in Chicago. There was no street address, only instructions that the package would be picked up. The express manager identified William Miller as the man who had sent the package. Banning immediately sent a telegram to the Chicago Police Department requesting that the package be intercepted.

The reply Banning received was disappointing. The package had already been claimed, and the Chicago police had no way of finding the addressee. They knew nothing of a Miss M. Connell. Banning was sure that whoever had picked up the package in Chicago was now in possession of the pickpockets' loot: gold and silver watches, chains, cameo brooches, and lockets, all lost forever to their rightful Canadian owners.

Banning also received a telegram from Allan Pinkerton, founder of the Pinkerton Detective Agency, which was headquartered in Chicago. Pinkerton had eyes and ears in the Chicago Police Department, and the name "Guerin" – mentioned in Banning's telegram – immediately caught his attention. Pinkerton's message to Banning read: "Paddy Guerin. Sneak thief and pickpocket. His pals are Ross

Salsbury and Billy Burke. Concerned in big jewellery robbery in Chicago. Have been in Canada since."

Detective Banning was certain that he had nabbed a gang of notorious American criminals. The Ottawa police kept the seven suspects in jail while detectives searched for more clues that might connect them to the pickpocket thefts or the Opera House robbery. Meanwhile, William Miller, who seemed to be the leader, hired Alexander Gibb, reputed to be the best criminal lawyer in Ottawa.

Three days after the Guerin party had been arrested, their case was heard by a county judge. The Opera House manager identified two men in the group as the pair who had disputed with him about ticket prices. But Gibb argued that it wasn't a crime for theatre lovers to make complaints about the cost of tickets. It wasn't his client's fault if some unknown person had pillaged the box office while he was talking to the manager. He said there was no proof that any of the money in the possession of any of his clients was stolen. Gibb deplored the injustice of people being kept in jail just because some policeman had found an allegedly stolen watch under a sofa cushion in a hotel.

Gibb further argued that the police had no real evidence connecting his clients to any crimes or criminals in the United States. The Chicago police hadn't asked the Ottawa police to hold the visitors. Allan Pinkerton's telegram didn't actually say that Paddy Guerin, Ross Salsbury, and Billy Burke were among the suspects Detective Banning had arrested. The Canadian Express manager's claim that William Miller had mailed a package with the name P. Guerin on it didn't necessarily mean that he *was* P. Guerin, and this was at best feeble evidence on which to hold him. He spoke movingly of the plight of citizens from a friendly nation "wrongfully and tyrannically imprisoned in the capital city of Canada."

Reluctantly, the magistrate had to let the seven Americans go. They lost no time in getting out of Ottawa on a train with connections to Chicago. Banning was certain that the swag from the Opera House robbery went with them.

Several days after the gang's departure, the Ottawa *Citizen* received a letter from a man who claimed to be the warden of an American prison, who said he was well-acquainted with Paddy Guerin. The writer said that he had seen the story about the Ottawa arrests in a press despatch. "Paddy Guerin", he said, "was just one of many aliases used by 'one of the cleverest sneak thieves in the country ... a notorious and skillful crook.'" He described

Guerin as an expert pickpocket, burglar, and "train worker" (a criminal who fleeced passengers on trains). He said the people Guerin travelled with were "a rattling mob of crooks who were always plying their vocation." The warden closed his letter with, "They are a bad lot. Send them to Kingston."

By the time the Ottawa *Citizen* received the letter, the suspects were long gone. No one would ever be able to prove if "Paddy Guerin" was involved with the rash of pickpocketing or the Opera House robbery, or if he had even been in Ottawa at all. But the name on the mysterious package sent from Ottawa to Chicago indicates that he was. "Paddy" was a name commonly applied to Irishmen in Canada and the United States. Guerin's first name was Edward or, as he preferred, Eddie.

Many years later, a former police reporter for the Ottawa *Citizen* who had covered the events recalled it all in an article published in the Toronto *Globe and Mail*. He named two of the gang members who were with Guerin as "Kid McManus" and "Chicago May". The reporter was mistaken. In 1878, Eddie Guerin had probably not yet met Kid McManus, and the girl who would become known as Chicago May was only eight years old. But by the time the *Globe and Mail* story appeared in 1932, those names had become internationally notorious and inextricably entwined because of a sensational robbery and an even more sensational escape story. Eddie Guerin became a figure of legend as the first man ever said to have successfully escaped from Devil's Island.

Shady Beginnings

The time and place of Eddie Guerin's birth are uncertain. He once claimed that he was born on a British ship at sea and that his surname was actually Fox. In his 1929 autobiography, *I Was a Bandit* (a book that unfortunately is full of embellishments), Guerin says that he was born to an Irish father and American mother in London, England in 1860, and that his family immigrated to the United States when he was very young. However, at the time of that publication, Guerin had a very important legal reason for maintaining his claim to have been born a British subject and not an American citizen. Oddly, he said that all records of his birth were destroyed in the Great Chicago Fire of 1871. A prominent Canadian journalist who investigated Guerin's life in the 1930s said that Eddie was born in Canada.

Guerin might even have been born earlier than 1860, though that date seems to have been accepted by many chroniclers of Eddie's story simply because it's the one he gave in his book. But when newspapers reported Guerin's death in 1932 (prematurely, as it turned out), they gave his age as 80, which meant he'd been born in 1852. Eight years later, when Guerin did in fact die, newspapers again reported his age as 80, in accordance with his claim to have been born in 1860. The discrepancy in birth years means that when Eddie was pulling robberies in Canada in 1878, he was either a youth of eighteen or a twenty-six-year-old man.

Wherever and whenever Guerin was born, he certainly grew up in Chicago, and it's certainly possible that his family could have arrived there by way of Canada. While Guerin was still a child, his father died, and the boy and his mother were poor. Eddie received little education. He learned to read and write but didn't like school. He preferred the rough-and-tumble life of the streets and the company of the toughs who hung out in pool halls. Eddie ran away from home and, during his adolescent years, he worked at any job he could find. He was a bell boy on a Lake Michigan passenger steamer and a "candy butcher" selling candy, peanuts, cigars, and newspapers on trains.

Then young Eddie got a job in Chicago as a Western Union telegraph boy. Running messages from the Western Union office to businesses and private homes opened up a new world of opportunity to a boy who loved loitering in pool halls and gambling but hated working for a couple of dollars a day. He took note of when houses and offices were unoccupied and could be burglarized. Eddie was only fifteen when he was arrested for stealing a box of silver cutlery and sent to Chicago's House of Correction.

There was nothing correctional about the first of Eddie Guerin's many incarcerations. He was locked up with hardened criminals who had broken just about every law in the book. Like all prisons of that time, the place stank. The food was vile, the guards brutal, and confinement in "the hole" with nothing but bread and water for extended periods of time was the punishment for most infractions. Guerin emerged from the place a year later feeling "vindictive toward the whole world."

Eddie fell in with criminals known as *yeggmen*. That was the slang term for "that vast traveling fraternity of crooks who used to get their living by various forms of robbery." The shady characters he associated with went by such monikers as Hans "the Dutchman" Schmidt, John the Mick, Sheeny Mike, Big Ed, Flash Billy, and Bill the Brute. For a while, Eddie joined the riffraff that trailed behind

Barnum's Circus as it toured the country. Wherever the circus went, there were crowds of people with pockets to pick. There were also suckers to be lured into fixed games of chance like thimblerig and "find the lady." Eddie's job was to watch out for cops while the crooks fleeced the rubes. He never let an opportunity to pull a burglary slip by, and sometimes he got caught and wound up spending time behind bars.

In Pittsburgh, Eddie and a yeggman named Joe Butts decided to rob the Pennsylvania Railway office. They drew the cashier away from his post, and while Joe engaged the man in conversation, Eddie looted the safe of $800. They made a clean getaway, but Joe got drunk in a saloon and loudly boasted of their exploit. Police heard of it and soon knew who the robbers were. Joe Butts managed to make himself scarce, but Eddie was arrested and sentenced to three years in the Allegheny State Prison. However, he and another man bribed a guard and escaped. Now Eddie Guerin was a fugitive "with a price on my head and liable to be shot at sight by any sheriff." He fled north to Toronto where, according to his memoirs, he "knew some people."

Even though he was in Canada, Eddie knew he had to lie low in Toronto. He learned that another Allegheny escapee known as Shoebox Miller had reached Toronto, but he then made the mistake of writing to a girlfriend in the United States. American police intercepted the letters and Toronto police arrested Shoebox. He was extradited and sent back to prison with years added to his sentence for escaping. Eddie didn't want to repeat Shoebox's error. He sent no letters home.

At first, Eddie found Toronto of the mid-1880s to be "a nice old-fashioned English city." He got a room in a boarding house and made his living by doing odd jobs and running an illegal faro table. He claimed in his book that during the Riel Rebellion, he tried to join a volunteer militia unit that was going west to fight, but "there were so many men available that they wouldn't have me ... I shall be greatly surprised if the French and the English ever settle down in peace and quietness."

Eddie was sometimes tempted to "bust a bank" in Toronto, but he didn't have a reliable partner. There was also the problem of the local police. "The Canadian bulls [police] were a different type altogether; you couldn't play any tricks on them, and they wouldn't listen to graft."

Before long, Eddie was homesick for cities like Chicago and Pittsburgh with their brothels, gambling dens, and saloons that were open day and night. "Saturday nights [in Toronto] everything closed down, and all you had to do on Sunday was go to church and listen to the sermons."

Eddie said in his book that after about a year, "Toronto began to pall on me ... I grew heartily sick and tired of the quiet life in Toronto."

Then one night at the faro table, Eddie met a couple of crooks from New York City. They were, as Eddie put it, "kindred souls". One of them said, "Ed, you're wasting your time in this downy old burg. You'd better come along with us to New York. We'll get some money together."

Soon Eddie was in the Tenderloin district of Manhattan, where his new friends introduced him to the denizens of the big city's underworld. He was back in his element: the world of thieves, prostitutes, gamblers, and cops and politicians who'd leave a working yeggman alone as long as he greased their palms.

Eddie was much happier in New York than he'd been in Toronto, but he and his pals took a trip to St. Louis to rob a bank. They were caught, and Eddie was quickly identified as an escapee from Allegheny. Eddie was shipped back to his old prison, where Shoebox Miller was still locked up.

Eddie was released in the fall of 1886 and went back to Chicago. He had hardly tasted free air before the incident occurred that would dramatically alter the course of his life. Eddie had an affair with the wife of a Chicago police detective named Tom Threehorn. The cuckolded husband came after him with a gun, and Eddie shot him.

As far as Eddie was concerned, it was self-defence. But he had shot a cop. If the man died, Eddie could wind up on the gallows. Threehorn did, in fact, survive, but Eddie hadn't stuck around to find out. Once again he fled to Canada, smuggled across the border by friends. But he no longer considered Canada a safe haven. If Canadian police learned that he was wanted, he would be arrested and extradited. Eddie had to put as much distance as possible between himself and the long arm of American law. With a small amount of money sent by family and friends, he made his way to Nova Scotia and boarded a ship for England.

Kid McManus and Chicago May

The London in which Eddie arrived in 1887 was one of the most dynamic cities in the world. It was the capital of a global empire, headquarters of the world's most powerful banks, and home to some of the wealthiest people on earth. But its sprawling, grimy, working-class districts were seething cauldrons of poverty and crime. Eddie was dead broke and friendless when he stepped off the ship, but he soon made contacts with shady characters who welcomed him into the London underworld. Though he was a newcomer, Eddie soon "got into the swim."

Chicago May

And just as soon, he floundered. Eddie and some of his new mates were arrested on charges of conspiring to rob a London post office. He spent several months (under a false name) in the old Millbank Prison, which he later described as a "foul, dirty, filthy hole" and "as cold as charity."

When Eddie was released, he thought it would be a good idea to get out of England for awhile. He joined a gang of crooks and crossed the channel to the Continent. According to his book, they visited Paris, Brussels, Monte Carlo, "and innumerable other places where you could pick up money in various ways which need not be enumerated here."

By that, Eddie meant robbery. Once again, things went badly for him. In the spring of 1888, Eddie and two companions robbed a bank messenger in Lyons of 250,000 francs ($50,000). They buried the loot in the woods outside of town and then returned to England. When the furor over the robbery had died down, Eddie quietly slipped back into France, retrieved the cash, and took it back to London where he converted it to pounds. However, while he was living the high life on his share of the plunder, an informer snitched to Scotland Yard. Eddie was arrested in July and extradited to France. A judge sentenced him to ten years in prison.

Eddie was behind bars again, this time in the prison of Rion, near Vichy. He didn't adapt well to the military-style regime imposed by the administration. He was frequently involved in fights with other inmates and confrontations with guards and so was subjected to harsh discipline. While Eddie was incarcerated, his mother died in Chicago. Eddie put in the full ten years, during which he learned to speak French. When his sentence was served, French authorities deported him to England.

Once more, Eddie was free but penniless. He either couldn't find a regular job because of his criminal background, or simply wouldn't knuckle down to honest employment. He made a meagre living working for a racetrack bookie. He spent a lot of time hanging out at a pub on Leicester Square that was popular with Americans, many of them his "kindred souls". It was there in 1899 that Eddie became acquainted with John "Kid" McManus.

Kid McManus was a notorious New York criminal, a "desperado by nature", as Eddie put it. In the underworld fraternity, he was reputed to be the best "box man" (safe cracker) in America. McManus had fled to England to escape Pinkerton detectives who were hot on his trail. He and Eddie knew each other by reputation and became good friends. It was through McManus that Eddie became entangled with the woman whose name would become synonymous with the term *femme fatale* –Chicago May.

She was born Beatrice Duignan (or Desmond) near Dublin, Ireland, in 1870, to a devoutly Catholic farm family. Her father was modestly successful and provided a comfortable home for his wife and children. But young Beatrice was headstrong and incorrigible. Her bad behaviour got her expelled from the convent school she attended. While still a teenager, she stole her father's life savings of sixty guineas, ran away from home, and bought passage on a ship to New York. Once in the United States, she began her quest for a life of fun, adventure, and easy money. She abandoned "Beatrice" in favour of "May".

May had no intention of slaving away in a factory or working as a humble domestic servant. She was strikingly beautiful, and quickly learned that men were willing to pay well for her sexual favours. She never admitted to engaging in prostitution but always referred to her liaisons with men as "dating".

In later years, May claimed that in the American West she married a young man named Dal Churchill. According to May's story, Dal was an outlaw who rode with the notorious Dalton gang. She said she cased banks for the bandits until Dal was caught and lynched by a vigilante mob. There is no evidence of a Dal Churchill ever being associated with the Dalton gang, or of a woman who cased banks for them.

Nonetheless, May arrived in Chicago sometime in the early 1890s, introducing herself as a young widow named Churchill.

The few honest occupations available for single women – laundress, cook, maid – still didn't appeal to May, so she went back to "dating". May was no common streetwalker. She was a clever, calculating criminal who learned how to manipulate men. She was a nimble-fingered pickpocket who could lift a man's wallet and watch in one passionate embrace.

There were a lot of tricks prostitutes used to steal or extort money from their clients. May sometimes worked with pimps known as "panel men". She would take a client into her room, where her partner was hidden behind a panel. When the client had taken his clothes off, the panel man would quietly snatch them out of sight. The pockets would be emptied, and the naked victim might even be obliged to arrange for an additional payoff before his clothing was returned and he could leave. May was particularly artful at fleecing "suckers" without actually having sex with them, thereby avoiding the possibility of pregnancy and disease. One ruse was to insist on payment in advance and then, on the pretext of going to the ladies' room, flee from the premises. But even if services were rendered, the client might find that it had cost him more than he had intended to pay when he opened his wallet later and found that his money had been replaced with newspaper clippings to give it the appearance of still being full.

May also prowled well-to-do social circles as a "badger". She would target married men who looked like good prospects for seduction. Any respectable husband, father, and moral pillar of the community foolish enough to succumb to her charms had to pay blackmail money to get out of the trap. The wealthier the mark was, the more his indiscretion would cost him.

Unlike the legions of unfortunate "soiled doves" who lived miserable existences selling their bodies for meagre financial return, May flourished. She wore expensive dresses, adorned herself with jewellery (much of it stolen), and lived in the finest hotels. Like Eddie Guerin, May got away with her lawlessness because of Chicago's corrupt administration and police department. She was arrested several times but rarely spent more than a night in jail.

In 1893, Chicago hosted the World's Fair. May plied her trade with the builders of the exhibition site, and then with the crowds of tourists that flocked to it. But business dropped when the fair ended and the suckers in the hotels went home. Feeling the need for a change of scenery, and perhaps because too many Chicago men were on to her games, May moved to New York City in 1894. There, amidst the shady characters of the underworld, she found that her reputation had preceded her. The crooks and prostitutes of New York gave her the name that would stick with her for the rest of her life, and beyond -- Chicago May.

New York was just as lucrative as Chicago had been. Chicago May "dated" rich and influential men, picked their pockets, and blackmailed them. But the New York police weren't as willing to turn a blind eye as the Chicago police. Sometimes May had to get out of town for a while if things got too hot for her. She would take trips to cities like Newark, New Jersey, and Detroit, Michigan, to lighten the pockets of rich gentlemen in the hotels. On at least one occasion, she crossed the border to Windsor, Ontario. She would return to New York after things had cooled down there for her.

In 1898, Chicago May made the first of several crossings from New York to London. These were like working vacations for her. The voyage across the Atlantic took about six days, depending on the weather. May always travelled first class so she could "date" and rob wealthy male passengers. In London she would do the rounds of the best hotels before sailing back to New York.

On one of these excursions in 1899, Chicago May met James Montgomery Sharpe, son of a wealthy New Jersey family. Believing that Jim was heir to a fortune, May married him. For once, May was the sucker. Jim turned out to be a wastrel and the family black sheep. He lived a life of dissipation, forged cheques, and whatever he stole from his mother. As a woman who had robbed her own father, May could hardly have passed moral judgement on Jim, but it became clear that he wasn't going to inherit the family fortune. After a short, stormy marriage, May left him.

May returned to London and established herself as a high-priced courtesan. She had an apartment on famous Bloomsbury Square and attended such fashionable events as the races at Ascot, where high society congregated and pockets were waiting to be picked. She had an affair with a British barrister that turned into a profitable blackmailing scam when May told the man, falsely, that she was pregnant with his child. One of Chicago May's favourite hunting grounds in London was Northumberland Avenue, which had several large hotels that were popular with well-to-do visitors. May even engaged local hoodlums to assist her with the old "panel man" trick.

Although Chicago May had one foot among the social elite, the other was firmly in the gutter, so it was inevitable that she would run into American criminals on the lam like Kid McManus. It was allegedly at the funeral of a notorious London criminal that McManus introduced May to Eddie Guerin. To Eddie, Chicago May was another "kindred spirit".

Eddie Guerin

Eddie Guerin and Chicago May took an instant liking to each other. For Eddie, the attraction was sex and the prestige of having a good-looking woman to wear on his arm as he strolled the streets of London and visited the night spots. May saw in Eddie a daring bandit who could provide her with money so she wouldn't have to work the hotels. Kid McManus took Eddie aside and warned him, "You leave that dame alone. She's dangerous. She'll rob you of everything you've got."

Eddie shrugged off the warning. "Don't worry about me, Kid," he said. "She can't get much because I've got nothing to lose." That, at least, is what Eddie later claimed was said.

The American Express Heist

It was true that Eddie had no money, but he and McManus were planning to make a "big smash". They spent two or three months looking for the right opportunity. Then early in 1901, they ran into a German-American named Gustav Muller, better known in the criminal fraternity as Dutch Gus. He was a trained engineer who had turned to robbery, using his expertise with explosives to blow open safes. Like Kid McManus, Dutch Gus had run into trouble with the Pinkertons in the United States and had relocated in London to make a "fresh start".

Dutch Gus had known Eddie slightly in the United States, but he first confided in Kid McManus about a job in Paris he'd been working on. He asked if McManus knew of a reliable third man they could bring in on the operation. McManus immediately recommended Guerin. Eddie was experienced, trustworthy, and could speak French.

Dutch Gus's target was the safe in the American Express Paris office on Rue Scribe. Gus had spent weeks casing the place and making plans. He'd arranged to have letters addressed to him mailed to the office so he'd have a legitimate reason to go inside, giving him the opportunity to study the layout. He'd also made friends with the young black man who was the caretaker. Aside from the caretaker, there were no security guards on the premises at night because the American Express officials believed their state-of-the-art safe was impregnable.

A return to France was potentially dangerous for Eddie, so recently a guest in a French prison. But the promise of a rich haul he could live on for years was irresistible to him – and to Chicago May. He also allegedly told May that he wanted revenge on the French for those ten years in Rion. Travelling separately, the bandits arrived in Paris where they registered under false names in different hotels. For three weeks, they pretended to be tourists enjoying the sights while they took turns watching the American Express office. They noted that the caretaker left every night at about seven o'clock to go to a café for a few drinks. He didn't return for two or three hours. At no time did they see any patrolling watchman or gendarme anywhere near the office.

One evening while the caretaker was having his nightly drink, Dutch Gus met him and managed to pickpocket his door key. He sneakily passed it to one of his partners who made a wax impression. Then Gus slipped the key back into the caretaker's pocket with him being none the wiser.

The robbery took place on the morning of April 27. Eddie claimed in his book that he left Chicago May in their hotel room, sleeping off a drunk. But in her own memoirs, May said that she was part of the team, standing as lookout.

Eddie joined Gus and McManus at a corner near the American Express office shortly after midnight. The other two had seen the caretaker return from his visit to the café and close the door behind him. They knew he'd go to his upstairs room to bed down for the night. With a few drinks in him, he'd fall asleep quickly.

The bandits waited in the shadows until 1:30. Then McManus crept up to the door and opened it with a key made from the wax impression. He slipped inside and was followed minutes later by Eddie and Gus.

McManus and Eddie went up to the caretaker's room and seized him as he lay asleep. Startled out of a boozy slumber, the man cried out in fear at the sight of the two masked men, one of whom held a gun at his head. McManus silenced him with dire threats of what would happen to him if he didn't shut up. Eddie stuffed a handkerchief into his mouth while McManus tied his hands and feet with rope. They stood watch over the terrified prisoner while, downstairs, Dutch Gus went to work on the safe.

Gus knew just how to apply dynamite so it would blow open a safe's door without destroying the contents. The one thing he could not prevent was the noise. Eddie and McManus heard a tremendous blast that seemed to shake the whole building. Eddie was sure that it must have awakened people for miles around and that, at any moment, the police would come charging in. But nothing happened. He and McManus went downstairs. The room was smoky and acrid with the smell of gunpowder. The safe door hung open, and Gus was hauling out stacks of loot.

The silence in the streets outside indicated that the sound of the explosion had been muffled by the thick stone walls. It would be hours before any American Express employees arrived at the office. The bandits decided to divide the swag right there. The safe held about $250,000, much of it in cheques and bonds. But around $20,000 was in cash. One by one, with their pockets stuffed, the robbers left the building. They all had their own plans for getting out of France. They had agreed to meet again in London.

News of the robbery soon hit the streets. According to the Paris newspapers, the caretaker said that the bandits were all Americans. The police had a suspect in custody: a youth who weeks earlier had broken into the American Express office one night and stolen some cash out of a few desk drawers. However, investigators quickly realized that this petty thief couldn't have pulled such an enormous heist.

Eddie was relieved that the police seemed to have no real idea who the robbers were. Nonetheless, he was cautious. He and Chicago May moved to a different hotel. They didn't realize that the police were already on their trail.

Several weeks earlier, Allan Pinkerton's son, Bill, head of the detective agency's Chicago office, had received a few tips from his underworld informants. He'd learned that Kid McManus and Dutch Gus were in London and that Gus had visited Paris. There was a rumour that Gus had been looking around in London for accomplices to help pull a big job. Pinkerton wired his contacts in the French Surete to be on the lookout for Americans who might be up to no good.

Surete detectives then learned from their own informers of some Americans who had been acting suspiciously. Days before the robbery, plainclothes policemen were following Eddie, Kid McManus, and Dutch Gus. They saw Gus buy rope in a chandler's shop near the American Express office, but they had no idea what he intended to do with it.

Surprisingly, the Paris detectives were unable to keep their subjects in sight on a regular basis. Either they were not well trained in the art of shadowing suspects or the experienced criminals were deliberately elusive in case they were being watched. Eddie, McManus, and Gus always separated after brief meetings and lost themselves in the crowded streets. The police didn't even know which hotels they were staying in. But as soon as the robbery was reported, the police had a good idea who was responsible.

Expecting the criminals to make a run for England, police watched the Paris railway stations and the Channel ports. At the Gare du Nord, they caught Dutch Gus as he was boarding a train. A detective recognized him as the man who had bought the rope at the chandler's shop – the same rope that had been used to tie up the caretaker. Gus even had a piece of the rope in his suitcase, along with loot from the robbery.

The police kept the news of Gus's arrest out of the papers. At Surete headquarters, they promised him a light sentence if he cooperated with them. Dutch Gus talked. He named Eddie Guerin and John "Kid" McManus as his accomplices. He told the police which hotels they were staying in. He even gave them the address of a flat McManus kept in London.

By that time Eddie and Chicago May had changed hotels. McManus, who was better than Gus at giving police the slip, had quietly made his way to Italy. Scotland Yard detectives watched his London flat in vain.

Eddie knew nothing of Dutch Gus's arrest. He wanted to lie low in Paris for a while and then go to some place where the police would be least likely to look for the robbers. But Chicago May wanted to get out of Paris and back to London as quickly as possible. Against his better judgment, Eddie gave in.

On May 1 they went to the train station. Chicago May was carrying most of the money. They climbed into a compartment and, as the train pulled away, Eddie stepped out into the corridor and lit a cigar. As he strolled up and down, two men approached him and asked in broken English if there was a buffet car on the train. Eddie replied in French that it was the last car. The two men suddenly seized him, slapped on handcuffs, and shoved him into an empty compartment. Eddie fit the description of one of the men the detectives were looking for, and they knew that Eddie Guerin could speak French.

Chicago May heard the scuffle and Eddie demanding to know what the "bloody game" was. To her surprise, no policeman entered her compartment. When the train stopped at Amiens, she saw the detectives take Eddie off in handcuffs. She stayed aboard and was soon in England – with the money.

On the train trip back to Paris, Eddie protested that the detectives had the wrong man. The officers said very little. It worried Eddie that they didn't interrogate him. "When the police ask you a lot of questions, they know nothing," Eddie wrote years later. "When they keep silent, they know a lot."

At the Paris police headquarters, Eddie was charged with the American Express robbery. He indignantly denied it, even when told that Dutch Gus had been caught and had confessed everything. A detective who had been on the Lyons robbery case years earlier confirmed that the suspect was in fact the notorious Eddie Guerin. "Ah, ah, it is the same old Eddie," he said.

Nonetheless, Eddie didn't think the police had any solid evidence connecting him to the robbery. He had only a small amount of cash on him at the time of his arrest. When he was confronted with Dutch Gus and was told that his partner had implicated him, Eddie scoffed, "He's a liar. He wants revenge because I took the woman he was after." (Dutch Gus had, in fact, made an advance on Chicago May, which she rejected).

The police didn't believe Eddie. They wanted to know what he'd done with his share of the money. He said he didn't know what they were talking about. "You have given it to the woman," his interrogator said. "Never mind, she shall be brought back here before long."

Eddie was held in solitary confinement in La Sante while the police tried to scour up enough evidence to convict him. So far, all they had was the dubious word of Dutch Gus. Eddie thought his chances of getting off were pretty good. Once he was released, he would hurry to London, track down Chicago May, and take back his cut of the swag. But May did the last thing Eddie and the French police expected her to do. Six weeks after Eddie had been captured,

May showed up at La Sante requesting permission to visit him.

It would bewilder Eddie for the rest of his life that a woman as experienced and as cagey as Chicago May would do something so foolish. She not only endangered herself, but she also all but doomed Eddie. Did she not realize that she was a suspect? Did she do it out of love? Probably not. It's possible that, for her own peace of mind, she needed to know just what Eddie had told the police.

Eddie never revealed exactly what he and May discussed during that prison visit. May said in her memoir that she gave Eddie $500 for his defense. After the visit, May went to the American consul in Paris and told him a tall tale about her unfortunate brother being arrested and held in prison simply because he had been foolish enough to fall in with bad companions. The consul called the police, who had only just then realized that the woman who had visited Eddie was the infamous Chicago May. By that evening, May was locked up in the La Roquelle women's prison.

The French police informed Scotland Yard that they'd found evidence on May that showed she had registered at the posh Bloomsbury Hotel in London and had rented a safe deposit box there. Detectives opened the box, but it was empty. A hotel employee said he had seen May take what appeared to be a packet of cheques out of the box and put it in her stocking. Scotland Yard investigators heard rumours that May had sold cheques to some underworld figures who were known to deal in such loot. They arrested a few suspects but couldn't find any of the cheques.

The London police also learned that when May first came back from France, she had been generously treating her friends to drinks, as though she had money to burn. Paris police discovered that when May returned to their city, before going to see Eddie in jail, she had paid for a grand drinking bout that attracted the sort of local riffraff that hung around cafes sponging off tourists. Everybody on the streets of London and Paris "knew" that Chicago May was spending money from the robbery.

The police still didn't know where May had stashed the bulk of the loot, but the fact that she had gone to see Eddie convinced them that she'd gotten the money from him. The French authorities were not about to let Eddie or May go. Under the Napoleonic Code of law, which said that a suspect had to prove innocence, they had the legal right to hold them.

Months passed, with Eddie and Chicago May sitting in their respective prisons, each wondering what the other might be telling the police. One day Eddie was taken before a magistrate who showed him a bundle of cheques that Scotland Yard had finally located and seized. "Here is the money you gave Chicago May," the judge said sternly.

"I never gave her any money," Eddie replied.

"Four people have been arrested in London passing these cheques," the judge said.

"Why don't you bring them over here?" asked Eddie. "They are probably the people who committed the burglary."

The frustrated magistrate sent Eddie back to his cell.

The day finally came for Eddie, Dutch Gus, and Chicago May to stand trial. Eddie and May stuck to their story that they had been together in their hotel room at the time of the robbery, that Eddie had not given May any money, and that Dutch Gus had made up a story out of jealousy. But Gus told the court everything he had told the police.

On its own, the testimony of a known criminal like Dutch Gus would have been very suspect, especially since the police had promised him leniency if he squealed on his partners. But that fact that Chicago May, Eddie

Guerin's lover, had been flush with money after the robbery, and then had gone to visit him in jail – circumstantial though that evidence may have been – convinced the jury that Gus was telling the truth. It took them only half an hour to reach a verdict of guilty for all three accused. Paris newspapers reported that Eddie and May "threw themselves into each other's arms."

Chicago May was sentenced to five years hard labour for knowingly receiving stolen money. Eddie Guerin, now a repeat offender in France, was sentenced to life in prison for robbery with violence. Dutch Gus, who thought he had a deal with the police, was stunned when the judge gave him the same sentence. May would serve her time in Montpellier Prison. But Eddie and Gus were horrified to hear that they would be transported to a penal colony in French Guiana, the most notorious of which was Devil's Island. As they were being led back to their cells, Eddie suddenly jumped at Dutch Gus and smashed him on the jaw before the guards could restrain him. Years later, Eddie lamented in his book, "In all probability I would have been acquitted had May kept out of the way."

The American Express robbery and the subsequent investigation and trial had received newspaper coverage around the world. Eddie Guerin and Chicago May gained international notoriety for a while. But once they had been packed off to prison and the drama was over, their names faded from the press. In 1902, Kid McManus, the only one of the robbers to successfully escape from France, was arrested by Canadian police after blowing up a safe in Ottawa. He was sentenced to ten years in the Kingston Penitentiary.

The Escape

For four years, the public heard nothing of Eddie Guerin. He had been swallowed up by the French penal colony system. Then in 1905, a sensational story hit American newspapers. Eddie Guerin was in the United States! He was the first man to successfully escape from infamous Devil's Island, the papers said. (French anarchist Clement Duval had escaped from the island in 1901, but the feat does not seem to have been well-covered in the English-speaking world).

Devil's Island had been in the news for several years because of the case of Captain Alfred Dreyfus, a French army officer of Jewish background who had been imprisoned on that "Isle of the Doomed" after being convicted of treason. It was eventually proven that the charges against Dreyfus were groundless and that he was a victim of anti-Semitism in the

French military. He was exonerated, sent back to France, and had his rank restored. In the meantime, Devil's Island and the horrific conditions under which prisoners lived received international scrutiny, to the embarrassment of the French government. In the eyes of the world, Devil's Island was one of the worst hell-holes on earth and a shameful example of inhumanity – which indeed it was.

The Guerin story, supposedly from Eddie's own lips, gave a first-hand account of a prisoner's brutal life on the island. Even more compelling was the description of Eddie's incredible escape. Told in the first person, the narrative gives a thrilling account of how Eddie and two other convicts slipped out of the prison compound, built a raft, and set off across shark-infested waters for the coast of Dutch Guiana (now Suriname). As they endured hunger, thirst, and the blazing tropical sun, Eddie's companions suddenly turned on him, believing he was carrying a secret hoard of money. Fortunately for Eddie, one of the turncoats was suddenly stricken blind by sunstroke and threw himself into the sea where he was devoured by sharks. Eddie pulled a revolver and kept the other man covered with it for three sleepless days and nights until they finally reached the mainland. (Devil's Island is actually only 14 kilometers off the coast).

In this story, Eddie says, "Having landed I told him he would have to fend for himself, and I struck out on my own. I followed the bank of a river through forests swarming with snakes and alligators, and at the end of three days, scarcely able to keep on my feet through hunger and fatigue, I came upon an encampment. I was soon surrounded by natives whose language was incomprehensible."

The story continues in this vein, with harrowing ordeals and hair-raising escapes, until Eddie finally reaches America. The tale of the man who escaped from Devil's Island had all of the lurid features of the pulp fiction that was so popular at the time. It sold newspapers and it made Eddie famous. But just how much of it was true?

The penal colony did not consist solely of Devil's Island. There were prison installations on nearby Ile Royale and Ile St. Joseph, and on the French Guiana mainland. Eddie and Dutch Gus spent time on Royale and St. Joseph, with Gus always keeping his distance from Eddie, who admitted he would have killed him if he ever had the opportunity. But they were never on Devil's Island.

Eddie was finally transferred to a prison on the mainland called Maroni, after the nearby Maroni River, which formed the border between French and Dutch Guinana. It was from there that he escaped. He had been planning it for a long time.

Some of the convicts were permitted to work outside the prison walls. Eddie managed to get himself assigned to a tailoring detail that worked in a house about a mile from the prison and close to the river. Every day he sat on the porch, stitching away with a needle and thread while a guard looked on. He frequently let his thimble go flying from his hand so that it landed in the brush. While the guard cursed him for being a clumsy fool, Eddie would go down and crawl into the bushes in search of the thimble. This happened so often over many weeks that the guard stopped taking notice. However long it took, Eddie always re-emerged with the thimble and went back to work.

Meanwhile, Eddie had been receiving money from family and friends. Bribery was the foundation of the penal colony's underground economy. Eddie paid to have an Italian prisoner who was a tailor by trade make him clothing with which to replace his conspicuous blue prison uniform. He also arranged for a former inmate, a Chinese man who lived in a shack near the river, to be paid to have a boat waiting.

On the day he planned to make a run for it, Eddie was wearing his escape clothes under his prison garb as he worked on the porch. He waited until dusk – a few fleeting moments between daylight and dark in the tropics – and then "accidentally" dropped his thimble. The guard didn't say a word as he stepped off the porch and dove into the bush.

As soon as he was out of the guard's sight, Eddie pulled off his prison uniform. He got a break when the guard went around to the other side of the building to relieve himself. Eddie didn't waste a moment. "I was off to the river as fast as my legs could carry me."

The boat was where it was supposed to be. Eddie slipped past river patrols and made it to freedom on the other side. But he wasn't the first to escape from Maroni. Other convicts before him had done it, though not all had been successful. With help from people he met along the way, Eddie crossed Dutch Guiana to British Guiana, where he found passage on a ship going to New York.

Eddie certainly suffered in the penal colony. About forty percent of the prisoners died from disease, malnutrition, overwork, and violence. Even though he didn't cross shark-infested seas on a raft with two treacherous companions, his escape was nonetheless a hazardous undertaking. The jungle was a hostile place, especially for a man who had known only city streets and the insides of prisons. Besides the natural dangers like poisonous snakes, quicksand, and maddening clouds of mosquitoes, there was the frightening possibility of getting lost in the wilderness. Native Indians, and ex-convicts who were forbidden to return to France, were paid bounties to hunt down escapees and bring them back - dead or alive. Runaways who were caught and returned alive faced harsh punishments, such as being chained to a log and forced to labour stark naked under the blazing sun.

In his autobiography, written many years after he had become legendary as "the first man to escape from Devil's Island", Eddie emphatically stated that he had never claimed to have been on Devil's Island. He denied having anything to do with the fantastic stories that appeared in the newspapers. He dismissed a story told by Chicago May after her release from prison, that she had arranged to have $5,000 smuggled to Eddie so he could bribe officials and have travelling money to get him home. "It's a nice romantic tale," Eddie wrote, "but totally devoid of truth." Eddie admitted that he did receive some money but wouldn't say from whom.

Eddie blamed an old friend named Pat Sheedy with inventing the Devil's Island story. Sheedy had once been the manager for heavyweight boxing champion John L. Sullivan and was well known among the shady characters who made money off prizefighting and gambling. He was equally at home in the company of rich "sporting men" and criminals like Eddie Guerin. Sheedy was an opportunist who grabbed at any chance to make money.

According to Eddie, Pat Sheedy was one of the first people to greet him when he finally arrived in the United States. After hearing Eddie's incredible tale of crime, imprisonment, and escape, Sheedy gave him some money to go to Chicago. Then Sheedy went to the American Press and sold them the wild tale about Eddie and Devil's Island, supposedly as told to him by Eddie himself, for $1,500.

The story spread rapidly, and in the telling and re-telling, different versions appeared. In one, Eddie shoots his two companions dead when they run out of food, the implication being that he resorted to cannibalism. Eddie complained that Sheedy's tall tale "pursued me like a ghost."

Of course, Eddie wouldn't have liked the idea of a story circulating in which he commits murder. But the question remains as to whether or not he actually collaborated with Sheedy on the original yarn. It apparently wasn't until the publication of his book in 1929 that Eddie denounced Sheedy's story. Even after that, the fictional account was still being accepted as Eddie's own testimony.

In 1934, Canadian journalist Gordon Sinclair travelled to French Guiana to investigate the story of "the only man who ever escaped from Devil's Island". In an expose that appeared in the Toronto *Daily Star*, Sinclair gleefully debunked the popular version of Eddie's escape. He quoted a passage in which Eddie claims that he and his companions hid in a swamp on Devil's Island for three days and nights, constructing a raft before putting out to sea. Sinclair pointed out, after visiting Devil's Island, that it is so small, a person could walk around its entire perimeter in half an hour. There is no swamp in which escapees could hide for three days while building a raft.

Sinclair examined Eddie's file at Maroni. Those documents showed that Eddie had, in fact, escaped from the mainland prison. Also, according to Sinclair, the papers identified Eddie as a Canadian. Sinclair called the whole Devil's Island escape story "bunk". He said that Eddie Guerin, "a Canadian skilled in the double cross and the snatch, a sneak thief and a forger ... has been playing the world for a sucker."

Still Wanted in France

However Eddie might have profited from his sudden fame in 1905, and whatever his official nationality, the publicity made him once more a hunted man. The French government wanted him back in the penal colony to serve out his life sentence. The French ambassador in Washington applied for extradition. It was rumoured in the capital that President Theodore Roosevelt would consider handing Eddie over to the French as an act of good will. Bill Pinkerton, who knew of Eddie's whereabouts in Chicago, could easily have had him picked up. But Pinkerton allegedly said that Eddie had suffered enough for what he had done and that he wouldn't send a dog to Devil's Island.

The Chicago police had a warrant for Eddie's arrest, but they dragged their feet in finding him. They were giving Eddie a chance to make a run for it. Since the United States was again unsafe for him, Eddie fled to an old refuge, Toronto. He stayed there for a few months, living under a false name on money sent to him by friends and "doing nothing that would bring me in conflict with the police."

Eddie finally decided that his only sanctuary lay in England. Once again he quietly left Canada. Meanwhile, due to poor health and a steady stream of pleas from her friends,

Chicago May had been released, after serving just two-and-a-half years of her sentence, and deported to England.

For a short period, Eddie worked in Leeds as a tailor, a trade he'd been obliged to learn in the penal colony. But, as he frankly admitted in his book, "I found it utterly impossible to stand the strain of slaving away in a tailor's workshop for two or three pounds a week, with nothing to do of a night except drinking around the public houses in the company of men I despised. So, toward the end of February, 1906, I threw down my needle and thread and made off to London, not caring very much what happened."

In London, Eddie was "scrambling for a living as best I could" – which probably meant that he was stealing. A few weeks after his arrival there, he met Chicago May in a pub. He wasn't sure if the meeting was purely accidental or if May had been searching for him.

For a long time Eddie had been nagged by a suspicion that Chicago May had somehow betrayed him while they were in jail in France, awaiting trial. His lawyer had told him at the time that May wanted to confess in hope of getting a lenient sentence. Considering that Dutch Gus had been handed a harsh sentence even after cooperating with the French police,

Eddie wondered if perhaps May *had* talked, only to be likewise double-crossed by the French authorities.

But that day in a London pub, as Eddie and May talked about old times and got drunk together on whiskey and sodas, Eddie's suspicions softened. Chicago May was still a very attractive woman. "I again took May to live with me," Eddie wrote later. If the old flame had indeed been rekindled, it wasn't destined to burn for very long.

The couple went to Aix-la-Chapell (Aachen), Germany, a spa town that drew tourists from all over Europe. Eddie and May weren't there for the famous waters but to ply their respective criminal trades. Eddie would steal, and Chicago May would do what she'd been doing for most of her life. However, it was one of her "dates" that turned the excursion into a disaster.

Eddie knew perfectly well what May did to make money, but evidently he had never actually witnessed her "at work". He became livid with jealousy when he saw her in the company of another man. May, who was also hot-tempered, said, "What's the matter with you? Can't I pick up an old guy without you kicking up a row? I've got to live somehow." After a fierce argument, May went back to London alone.

Eddie returned to London around the end of April. A woman named Emily Skinner, who was a mutual friend of Eddie and May, told him of a treacherous plot in which she said May had asked her to participate. According to Emily, May had told her before the trip to Aix-la-Chapell that she no longer loved Eddie. She was going with him only because she was sure he would get his hands on some money. When they returned to London, May wanted Emily to help her get Eddie drunk and then rob him. After that, they would tell Scotland Yard where Eddie could be found so the police could turn him over to French authorities. Emily had a letter, supposedly written by Chicago May, as proof.

Emily might have been telling the truth, and the letter might have been genuine. However, it was also possible that Emily had become infatuated with Eddie herself and was jealous of May. Whatever the case, Eddie believed Emily's story. As far as he was concerned, he'd been right all along to suspect May of betraying him. Now Eddie wanted revenge.

With Emily's compliance, Eddie and May met in a hotel bar. The three of them spent a few hours drinking. Eddie seemingly made up with May over the trouble in Aix-la-Chapell, and they agreed to let bygones be bygones.

They left the bar about midnight and went to Emily's flat. Emily found some excuse to go out again and left May alone with Eddie. He closed the door behind her and locked it, and then he dropped all pretenses.

In a fury, Eddie confronted May with her supposed treachery. May denied it. She said she would never break the "code of criminals" by handing him over to the police. But Eddie was too consumed with rage to listen.

Calling May "a dirty damned traitress of the worst type", Eddie tore off her clothing, which he said he had paid for. Then, in Eddie's own words, "I ... gave her a thrashing, which I wager she still remembers, and then flung her outside the door."

"Now," I shouted after I had finished with her, "you can go and tell the police all about me and tell them to go to hell with you. I'm leaving the country now, and I don't give a curse what happens."

After beating May up, Eddie went to his own lodgings. Nobody could say that Chicago May wasn't tough. She had been dealing with pimps, crooks, dirty cops, and men who were hard cases all her life. Aside from Emily's questionable letter, there was no evidence that she had ever been an informer. Once, when a

Scotland Yard detective had tried to convince her to squeal on her friends, May smirked, "Say, ain't you the wise guy."

But now Chicago May was afraid of Eddie Guerin. She owned a gun, but shooting Eddie would only land her back in prison – or maybe even on the gallows. She could flee back to the United States, but he might follow her. May's best hope for her personal safety and peace of mind lay in having the police get Eddie out of London and out of her life for good. After Eddie had stormed off, May dragged herself, battered and naked, back into Emily's flat. She found some clothes and then went to the Tottenham Court Road police station. The telephone wires linking police stations all over London were soon humming, and Scotland Yard contacted the Surete in Paris.

Eddie hadn't believed that Chicago May would go to the police. After all, she was a crook like him and preferred to keep as far away from the law as possible. So he was surprised when, two days after his violent confrontation with May, a friend told him that the police were looking for him. The friend had even more disturbing news. It was reported in the French newspapers that Eddie Guerin, the escapee from Devil's Island, was in London and would be extradited to France as soon as the British police picked him up.

Eddie was stunned. He'd been sure that enough time had passed for the French to have lost interest in him. He hurried to a news agent's shop where he often bought French newspapers. May must not have known where Eddie was living, or the police would already have arrested him. But she evidently knew where he bought his papers, because the police were watching the shop. Eddie had just purchased the latest editions of *Petit Parisien* and *Le Matin* when three Scotland Yard detectives seized him and clapped him in handcuffs.

Locked in a cell at the Tottenham Court Road police station, Eddie cursed Chicago May. But he had much larger problems than an angry ex-girlfriend. The superintendent of the police station told him that the French government had officially applied for his extradition. The awful spectre of the penal colony loomed before him.

Eddie was transferred to the Bow Street police station where a magistrate presided over the extradition hearing. The lawyer representing Eddie failed to impress the magistrate with his arguments on Eddie's behalf. The court's ruling was that extradition be granted. The lawyer told Eddie it would be no use appealing the magistrate's decision. It looked as though Eddie would soon be on his way to French Guiana. However, if the French authorities were rubbing their hands together in anticipation of getting hold of Eddie Guerin again, they were about to be disappointed.

While Eddie lay in a cell in Brixton Prison, expecting every day to be hauled across the Channel to France, a solicitor named G.W. Ricketts was pleading his case with Richard Muir, one of the most famous barristers in Britain. Whether serving as crown prosecutor or counsel for the defense, Muir was a formidable courtroom fighter. If anybody could save Eddie, it was he. But would he represent a lowly hoodlum like Eddie Guerin?

Eddie couldn't afford to hire such high-priced legal talent as Muir. But one thing he did have in his favour was publicity. The arrest of the man who had escaped from Devil's Island had made headline news. It was followed by lurid accounts of his betrayal by the infamous Chicago May and articles about the notorious penal colony in which an unjust French government had imprisoned innocent Captain Dreyfus. The British public saw Eddie as an underdog hero.

Muir realized that the eyes of the nation would be on the Guerin extradition case. People would be watching to see if a British court, representing King Edward VII and the highest ideals of legal justice in the civilized world, would send a man to the horrors of Devil's Island. And there was something else that Muir came across as he examined Eddie's record, something that sent his legal mind spinning. Eddie should *not* have been extradited in 1888!

Under certain clauses of Britain's Extradition Act, British subjects could be ruled unextraditable. Muir didn't particularly like Eddie Guerin, but he did believe in British law. He was determined that the mistake would not be repeated, especially with Devil's Island as Eddie's ultimate destination. Muir felt that the place was too inhumane, even for a scoundrel like Eddie. He thus began a legal fight that would last over a year and become a landmark case in British judicial history.

The problem lay in proving that Eddie Guerin was in fact a British subject. Because Eddie had grown up in Chicago, everyone assumed he was an American citizen. But no record of his birth could be found, and he himself had always been vague about where he'd been born. Up until Muir raised the question, Eddie had never made any claim to being a British subject. (It would be almost thirty years before Gordon Sinclair claimed to have seen evidence that Eddie was Canadian).

However, now that Eddie's freedom, and quite likely his life, depended on his being a

British subject, he embraced the Union Jack. He claimed that in his "extreme boyhood" in Chicago, he was known as Cockney Guerin because of an accent he had long since lost. That, he said, was proof that everybody regarded him as a Londoner.

Of course, Muir needed more substantial evidence. The key was Eddie's father. Edmund Guerin had been born in Ireland, making him a British subject. He eventually moved to Chicago, but he never became an American citizen. Muir's contacts in Chicago found no evidence that Edmund had ever voted in an election, for which he would have had to prove American citizenship. Muir argued that, to his dying day, Edmund Guerin had been a British subject, and therefore so were his children, regardless of where they'd been born.

The Crown prosecutor pointed out that pertinent records had been destroyed in the Great Chicago Fire. He challenged Muir to prove that Edmund had never become an American citizen. Muir countered by saying that Edmund had been born a British subject, and the onus was not on the defense to prove that he *hadn't* changed his nationality, but on the Crown to prove that he *had*.

On June 14, 1907, the court ruled in Eddie's favour. He was a British subject and could not be extradited. He was released immediately. "I felt I had never done so much for a man in all my life when I saw the change in Guerin's face," Muir remarked later. "It lit up with the most unspeakable relief I have ever seen."

When Eddie walked out of the building, a crowd of reporters awaited him. He pushed past them and jumped into a cab. "I had my freedom, which was the only thing in the world that mattered," Eddie recalled in his book. "I wasn't even thinking of Chicago May." But May had certainly been thinking of Eddie.

May had been disappointed when Eddie wasn't immediately packed off to France when he was arrested. He would know who had informed on him, and she was afraid of what he would do to her if he ever got out of jail. She thought it would be a good idea to get out of London, just in case. In 1906, a major diplomatic event called the Pan-American Conference was being held in Rio de Janiero, Brazil. The hotels there would be full of dignitaries from all over the Western world. May borrowed some money from a friend and boarded a ship bound for Rio.

For several months, while Eddie was fighting for his freedom in court, Chicago May was working the Rio hotels: seducing, robbing, and blackmailing wealthy and politically influential men. She caught the attention of Sir Sidney Hamilton Gore, the British Consul General in Argentina. He had a reputation among the elite of being something of a rebel – a man who liked to shock the sensibilities of his peers.

Sir Sidney took May as his escort to an exclusive ball. She was one of the most splendidly dressed women there. But as her name was passed around the room in whispers, the reaction of the other guests was muted disgust. Sir Sidney had brought into their midst a woman who was not only a lowly commoner, but also a notorious whore. They were outraged, which of course was what Sir Sidney had intended. The hostility was lost on May, who was as awed by her elegant surroundings as Cinderella at the royal ball.

Sir Sidney might have taken cynical delight at the discomfort he'd caused his snobbish colleagues, but his indiscretion didn't go over very well with his superiors in the Foreign Office. Sir Sidney apparently didn't give a damn what anyone thought. He and May went on a drinking spree that lasted several days. According to May, he even proposed to her. Then one afternoon, they caused an ugly scene in a bar when May complained that another man had insulted her. The disgraceful public drunken display involving a British titled gentleman who was a representative of His Majesty's government caused Sir Sidney even more problems with the Foreign Office.

Sir Sidney was undoubtedly a deeply troubled man long before he ever met Chicago May, but for her, the timing would be most unfortunate. Soon after the sordid incident in the bar, Sir Sidney shot himself in the head in his hotel room. It became part of the legend of Chicago May that she had driven an infatuated English aristocrat to suicide. May might have grieved over the sudden, tragic death of Sir Sidney, but she quickly boarded a ship for England, allegedly after a brief stay in a Rio jail.

While Chicago May was carousing around Rio, thousands of miles away in Brixton Prison, Eddie met a young man who called himself Cubine Jackson. His real name was Charles Smith. He was an American-born ne'er-do-well who had gone under several aliases and had a long criminal record. His travels had taken him as far as South Africa, where he'd been jailed and then deported for being a house-breaker. When Eddie met him in Brixton, Smith was awaiting trial on a burglary charge.

Eddie became friendly with "Cubine Jackson". He spent long hours talking about his adventures. In the lonely monotony of prison, there wasn't much else to do, and an apparently sympathetic ear was always welcome. Whenever Eddie came to the matter of Chicago May, he bluntly told his new friend that if he ever got the chance, he would kill her. "Jackson" agreed that a woman who had done what May had done should be made to pay for it.

As it turned out, the charge against "Jackson" was dismissed. Before leaving the prison, he agreed to do a job for Eddie. He would find Chicago May and give her a beating, perhaps disfigure her face – compliments of Eddie Guerin. At least, that was Charlie Smith's story.

Eddie and Chicago May: The Showdown

Once he was out of jail, Smith dropped the "Cubine Jackson" alias. He did find Chicago May, but instead of assaulting her, he fell under her spell. At thirty-five, May was ten years older than Charlie, but to him she was an enchanting, exotic woman. The attraction was mutual. May saw in Charlie a handsome, virile young man in whose company she could forget that she was approaching middle age. He had two other attributes that were important to May. Charlie was a criminal who could provide her with money. In her memoirs, she described him as "a high grade prowler". She also saw him as a protector, the sort of man she would need if Eddie Guerin won his case against extradition.

On June 14, even before the newspapers hit the streets, the news swept through London that Eddie Guerin, the man from Devil's Island, had won and was free. Chicago May was terrified. She knew it was only a matter of time before Eddie came looking for her. Either she or Charlie decided that they would get Eddie first.

The cab Eddie caught after his courtroom victory took him to the Provenance Hotel, where Emily Skinner and a crowd of friends waited to celebrate. The party lasted the better part of twenty-four hours, with the beer and liquor flowing freely. On the morning of June 15, Eddie and Emily left the hotel and walked toward the Russell Square tube (subway) station. They stopped in front of a shop, and Eddie waited while Emily went in to buy a newspaper.

A cab drove by, and a woman's voice cried, "There he is!" The cab stopped suddenly, and a man and a woman jumped out. The man pulled a pistol out of his coat and opened fire on Eddie while the woman screamed, "Kill him!"

Eddie ducked and dodged, trying to avoid the fusillade, but a bullet struck his foot. He fell, howling with pain, while the would-be assassin tried to make his escape. Some men who had witnessed the shooting chased him as he ran down the street, but stopped when he turned and threatened them with the gun. A pair of patrolling bobbies ran to the scene. The gunman pointed the pistol at them and pulled the trigger, but it only clicked. The gun was empty. The constables tackled the man and subdued him. The suspect, Charlie Smith, was drunk, which probably accounted for his incredibly bad aim.

Chicago May hadn't even tried to run. She stood there exchanging curses with Eddie while he sat bleeding on the sidewalk. More bobbies arrived and May was arrested. She was found to have a knife in her possession. Charlie and May were hauled off to jail, charged with attempted murder and wounding with deadly intent.

Once again, the misadventures of Eddie Guerin, invariably described as the escapee from Devil's Island, and his former lover, the scarlet woman called Chicago May, filled newspaper columns. In the aftermath of the shooting and during the subsequent trial, they became one of the first examples of criminals whom the press turned into "celebrities". In coffee houses and pubs, and in gentlemen's clubs and upper class salons, people talked about the case and took sides. Some were for Eddie, who had been betrayed by a treacherous Delilah. Others sympathised with May, who had no choice but to defend herself from a brute who had sworn to kill her.

Eddie was the main witness for the prosecution – an unusual situation for him. He claimed in his book that while he was reluctant to testify against Chicago May and Charlie, he did so because he was forced by law to give evidence. He wrote later, "I would have preferred to settle with them at my own time and in my own place."

Charlie was defended by prominent London barrister Huntley Jenkins. Chicago May's lawyer was Arthur Newton, who in 1895 had unsuccessfully defended Oscar Wilde against charges of immorality. Jenkins and Newton put up a dramatic courtroom fight in which they attacked the character of Eddie Guerin and focused on the fact that he had threatened Chicago May. But Eddie was the one who had been shot in the foot.

The jury found Charlie and May guilty. She was sentenced to fifteen years in prison. He was sentenced to life, with a provision that, after twenty years of good behaviour, he could be deported to the United States. Charlie was dragged from the courtroom cursing Eddie, the judge, and everyone else. Chicago May laughed.

"I laughed and laughed," May wrote later, "so as to show the minions of the law that they hadn't broken my spirit and to show my sympathy for Charlie, to encourage him."

In the aftermath of the trial, Eddie became, in his words, "a veritable lion of the underworld." Newspapers wanted to interview him and photographers hounded him for pictures. Eddie made them all pay for the privilege. He managed to save enough money to open a little tobacco and candy shop in London's West End.

In March 1908, Kid McManus was due to be paroled from Canada's Kingston Penitentiary where he'd been serving time for the Ottawa robbery. The French government, still smarting over its failure to get its hands on Eddie Guerin a year earlier, applied to the Canadian government for extradition. McManus was moved from Kingston to the St. Vincent de Paul Penitentiary in Laval, Quebec, while Canadian authorities decided whether to hand him over to the French or deport him to the United States. Working on Kid's behalf for deportation were two influential Americans: Senator Timothy Sullivan and Sheriff "Big Tom" Foley of New York. They had befriended

McManus years earlier when he had been the proprietor of a popular New York saloon.

The legal fight over McManus lasted until early May, when the American Express Company withdrew all charges against him. Company officials might have been persuaded by Sullivan and Foley that prosecuting McManus in France could be costly, with an uncertain chance of success. There was also the prospect of him being sent to Devil's Island, which would result in negative publicity. Since the victim of the Paris robbery had dropped the charges, the French government withdrew the application for extradition. Kid McManus was deported to the United States.

Chicago May was released in 1917 after spending ten years in the Aylesbury Prison for Women in Buckinghamshire. Because she had never divorced Jim Sharpe, she was still legally the wife of an American citizen, and therefore officially American herself. The British government ordered her deported to the United States.

When Chicago May walked out of the prison, she tried to carry herself with pride and dignity. In spite of her prison ordeal, at forty-five, she was still a woman who turned men's heads. The police constable assigned to escort May to the ship allegedly took one look at her and exclaimed, "Blimey! A bit battered, but still in the ring!"

Nonetheless, she wasn't the Chicago May of old. Prison had broken her health. Back in the United States, she found that her criminal record and bouts of illness made it impossible for her to find honest employment to support herself. She fell back into prostitution, but she was no longer a high-priced courtesan. She had to work with pimps who sold her services for as little as $10.

Chicago May found some redemption around 1927 when Detroit Police Chief August Vollmer met her in a jail infirmary. Vollmer was an idealist who believed that even the hardest career criminals could turn their lives around. He suggested to May that when she got out of jail, she try writing about her life. May took that advice and wrote a series of candid articles about her career as a thief, blackmailer, and con artist, which she sold to the *Weekly American*. The success of those articles led to May writing her autobiography, *Chicago May: Her Story*, which was published in 1928. Sadly, May's failing health didn't allow her to enjoy fame as an author for long. She died in a Philadelphia hospital after undergoing abdominal surgery on May 30, 1929.

The year 1929 also saw the publication of Eddie Guerin's autobiography, *I Was a*

Bandit. Eddie's attempt to go straight hadn't lasted very long. Running the tobacco and candy shop bored him. It also annoyed Eddie that Scotland Yard detectives were always poking around on suspicion that he was using the shop as a "blind" – a cover for criminal activities. He finally sold the business and went back to his old ways.

In 1917, Eddie was caught stealing jewellery from a hotel room in Brighton and sentenced to two years in Portsmouth Prison. Such was to be the routine for the remainder of his life, in and out of jail for mostly petty theft. He was out of jail when he wrote *I Was a Bandit,* almost certainly with the help of a professional ghost writer. Throughout the text, Eddie continually returns to the "crime does not pay" theme and warns young men not to make the mistakes he made.

But Eddie couldn't follow his own advice. After the book's publication, he was in jail as often as he was out of it. He complained that the police framed him for robberies he hadn't committed; that he was persecuted because of his past. There might have been some truth to that. Any arrest that involved the man who had escaped from Devil's Island was deemed worthy of newspaper space.

In 1936, Eddie received a windfall of $3,500 from the estate of a half-sister who had died in Chicago. The money didn't last long, most likely squandered in Eddie's favourite pastimes of drinking and gambling. Two years later, Eddie was arrested in a London post office for "loitering with criminal intent." A magistrate banished him from London for three years.

Eddie spent his final years in Manchester, a penniless old crook living by whatever means he could. His old robbery partner Kid McManus had disappeared after being deported from Canada to the United States. Dutch Gus had probably died in French Guiana. The last time Eddie had seen him, Gus was wracked with fever. And his old lover-foe Chicago May was dead.

Eddie Guerin died in a Manchester hospital on December 3, 1940, and was laid in a pauper's grave. The Battle of Britain was raging as German bombers pounded British cities, but newspapers around the world reported on Eddie's passing. Incorrigible as he was, and regardless of whether he was American, British, or Canadian, Eddie Guerin would have a place in legend, deservedly or not, as the first man ever to escape from Devil's Island.

Clan-na-Gael: Attack on the Welland Canal

At 6:20 pm on Saturday, April 21, 1900, two strangers got off the Niagara, St. Catharines & Toronto train when it made its regular stop at the little town of Thorold on the Welland Canal. Each man carried a small valise. There was nothing unusual about them, and nobody paid them any particular attention. But they were seen by enough witnesses for their movements to be accurately reported later.

Instead of heading for Thorold's business district, as most visitors did, these men walked a short distance along the railway tracks and then cut over to the canal bank. They followed it until they arrived at Lock 24. There, they were seen to duck behind a storehouse. A few minutes later they reappeared. One man headed for the lower gate of the lock and the other for the upper gate. At the lower gate, the first man tied a rope to his valise, lit a fuse, and then lowered the valise about ten feet so that it hung against the side of the gate. He then hurried to his companion at the upper gate and was heard to say, "Hurry up and drop it!" Moments later, a second valise with a burning fuse was dangling from a rope against a lock gate.

At about 6:30, a tremendous explosion shattered the quiet of little Thorold when the dynamite in the valise at the lower gate went off. It was followed less than three minutes later by a blast at the upper gate. The shock waves shattered windows throughout Thorold. People heard the explosions in Port Dalhousie, five miles down the canal, and in St. Catharines, eight miles the other way. Fortunately, no one was near enough to the blasts to be killed or seriously injured.

The lower gate had a hole blown in its woodwork and considerable damage done to its ironwork, and both gates were almost sprung. But instead of giving way, the gates settled upright on the bottom of the canal and held the water back. Had the act of sabotage succeeded, all the weight of a mile-long stretch of water between Locks 23 and 25 would have surged down toward Port Dalhousie, causing extensive damage to the canal and major flooding. Even as residents of Thorold rushed to the scene of the crime, rumours were being hatched as to who was responsible. This wasn't the first time the Welland Canal had been attacked. Its strategic role as a transportation link to the heart of North America made it a potential target for political and economic reasons.

When the Welland Canal opened in 1829, connecting Lake Erie and Lake Ontario, it ended the long period during which the western end of Lake Ontario had been a dead end for commercial shipping due to the unnavigable Niagara River. Ports throughout the Great Lakes now had a direct route to the St. Lawrence River and the Atlantic Ocean. That took a lot of business away from the famous Erie Canal, which connected Buffalo at the eastern end of Lake Erie with New York City. There had been a sense of resentment in Buffalo ever since. But that wasn't the cause of the first attack on the canal.

On September 9, 1841, a bomb shattered a gate on Lock 37 at Allanburg. Benjamin Lett, the principal suspect, was an admirer of William Lyon Mackenzie, though he hadn't actually participated in the 1838 Upper Canada Rebellion. However, he had been implicated in several crimes, including murder, and the bombing of the monument to Sir Isaac Brock at Queenston on April 17, 1840. Lett's bomb had shut down the canal for only twelve hours. He was captured in Buffalo and served time in prison. In 1858, Lett died in Illinois under mysterious circumstances. His brother claimed he'd been poisoned by "Tory" agents from Canada.

The Mackenzie Rebellion and Benjamin Lett were distant memories in 1900, but hard feelings toward the Welland Canal still lingered in Buffalo. The bombing happened just a few days before the canal was scheduled to open for the season. Coming down the lakes were ships with holds full of grain that had been stored in western silos all winter. Dock workers in Buffalo who earned their money shovelling grain from cargo ships to Erie Canal barges were angry that American vessels carrying American grain would pass them by in favour of the Canadian route. There was a strong suspicion that they had tried to blast the Welland Canal out of operation.

One other rumour passed through the crowd gathering on the canal bank as the smoke from the explosions drifted across the countryside: "Pro-Boerism!", as the Toronto *Globe* put it. Since October of 1899, Britain had been embroiled in the Boer War (now called the South African War). Canadian volunteers had already sailed off to fight for Mother England. Internationally, there was a lot of sympathy for the Boers (farmers of Dutch descent), who were battling the might of the British Empire. Could it be that Boer supporters in the United States were behind the bombing?

An Ontario police branch known as the Staff of Border Officers was notified by telegraph. That evening, in Niagara Falls, Detective William Mains organized search parties of county constables and civilians sworn in as special constables. A heavy rain had started, but as news spread, a large number of volunteers turned out to join the posse. The two suspects had last been seen running down the road from Thorold toward Niagara Falls. Detective Mains was certain they would try to cross the border into the United States, so he sent groups of men out to cover the entire Niagara Frontier. They had only sketchy descriptions of the suspects to go on.

At nine o'clock, a Thorold constable named Clark rode into Niagara Falls and reported that as he passed through the village of Stamford, he had seen two men who fit the descriptions of the suspects. Mains, Clark, and a police officer named Walsh immediately headed down the road toward Stamford. They had just reached the edge of the community at 9:30 when they saw the two men coming up the road toward them.

In the rain and darkness, the three policemen easily concealed themselves. When the suspects drew near enough, the officers pounced on them and subdued them before they could show any resistance. It was fortunate that the men were taken completely by surprise, because each had a loaded revolver in his coat pocket.

At the police station in Niagara Falls, the prisoners identified themselves as John Walsh, 27, a bartender from Washington D.C., and John Nolan (also spelled Nolin), 33, a machinist from Philadelphia. Thorold residents who saw Walsh and Nolan in the Niagara Falls jail said that they had seen the same men in town several times in the week before the explosions. They always seemed to be loitering near the canal, and they crossed and re-crossed the bridge several times a day, always in the company of a third man.

Acting on a description given by witnesses, and perhaps on information provided by the prisoners, voluntarily or not, Mains arrested a man who had registered at Niagara Falls's Rosli Hotel as Karl Dullman (also spelled Dallman) of Washington D.C. Dullman was a stout, well-dressed man of about fifty who had a lot of cash on him. He refused to answer any questions police asked him. Detective Mains's investigators learned that Dullman frequently crossed the border, drank a lot, and spent money freely as he presented himself as a generous friend to all he met. Then Mains was informed, to his surprise, that Canadian and American customs agents had been watching Dullman, Walsh, and Nolan as suspected opium smugglers.

Police in Niagara Falls, New York, searched a hotel room where Walsh and Nolan had been staying and found dynamite fuses, the first hard evidence linking them to the crime. On Sunday, April 22, Canadian authorities received a tip that two hundred men from Buffalo intended to cross the border and rush the jail to liberate the prisoners. Niagara Falls Mayor Robert P. Slater, fearful that local police wouldn't be able to handle such a mob, called on the militia. Twenty-five men of the 44th Battalion with loaded rifles and fixed bayonets surrounded the jail. Special police deputies were sent to patrol the canal and guard key locations, such as the railway tunnel under the bridge near Merritton. More police beefed up security at the border crossings. The local telephone exchange, which usually closed at six pm on Sunday, was kept open all night in case of an emergency.

No mob from Buffalo came storming across any of the Niagara bridges. But heightened suspicions that Buffalo businessmen or labour organizations were behind the blasts swept away rumours of Boer sympathizers. Long-standing resentment against the canal had been fuelled by the recent construction of grain elevators in Port

Colborne and Montreal. Men who depended on the Erie Canal for profits and jobs foresaw even more of the vital grain traffic going to the Canadians.

On April 23, the Toronto *Globe* reported: "The general impression is that the prisoners are not Boer sympathizers, but only three of a gang of dynamiters operating probably as hirelings of capitalists or labor to cripple the Welland Canal, with a view to diverting the traffic of the upper lakes from Montreal to Buffalo. Several of the gang are still at large, and another attempt will probably be made to further injure the canal. Chief [Thomas] Young [of the Niagara Falls Police Department] and Detective Mains placed a strong guard of deputies on the jail last night and today where the prisoners were locked up."

However, in spite of all the rumours and speculation, one man didn't agree that Buffalo capitalists or labour agitators were responsible for the bombing. The day after the attack, the Attorney General of Ontario assigned Chief Inspector John Murray of the Ontario Criminal Investigation Department to take charge of the case. He was a veteran investigator who would go down in the annals of Canadian crime as Canada's "Great Detective." Murray said that until he had a chance to look into the events, he had no definite theory of his own on who was responsible, but he thought that Fenians probably had a hand in it.

That stirred up memories of 1866, when a Fenian force made up of Irish-American veterans of the Union Army, battle-hardened by the Civil War, invaded Canada. Their purpose was to gain Ireland's independence from British rule by capturing Canada. The Fenians clashed with Canadian militia at Ridgeway, across the Niagara River from Buffalo, in what would be the last pitched battle fought on Canadian soil. The invasion was a failure, and although concerns about Fenian activity lingered long after the events of 1866, they never again posed a serious threat to Canada. However, time would prove that Chief Inspector Murray wasn't far off in his initial suspicion.

By the time Murray arrived in Niagara Falls on the train from Toronto, the prisoners had been moved to the county jail in Welland. Murray interviewed local police officers and then went to Welland to question the suspects. It didn't take him long to conclude that Dullman was the leader.

Dullman, Nolan, and Walsh had already engaged lawyers but had spent no more than a few minutes with them by the time Murray arrived. In a move that shocked the prisoners and their counsellors, but which was perfectly legal at the time, Murray ordered that the accused were to have no further communication with their lawyers until after a preliminary investigation had been concluded. Murray told the lawyers that if they wanted to speak to their clients, they would have to apply to the Attorney General for permission. The lawyers had already advised the prisoners "to preserve a rigid silence."

The initial police court hearing was held on April 24 in the Welland town hall before Magistrate Alexander Logan. T.D. Cowper, the County Crown Attorney for Welland, was the prosecutor. F.C. McBurney represented Nolan and Walsh, and A.F. Crow stood for Dullman. The little courtroom could seat only a hundred people and was so crowded with curious spectators that there was barely room for the prisoners to line up in front of the magistrate's bench. More people were gathered outside, eager to hear any bit of news.

After the charges had been read, Cowper requested that the prisoners be remanded for eight days. Before anyone else could say a word, Dullman stood up and said, "I trust we will not be remanded. As a citizen of the United States, I demand that whatever evidence there may be against me be produced at once."

Mr. Crow followed Dullman's outburst with a request for bail. Cowper explained that the remand was necessary for the Crown to have time to gather evidence and that bail was out of the question because the accused would likely flee across the border. In spite of arguments from Crow and McBurney, the remand was granted and bail was denied. Dullman, Nolan, and Walsh would remain behind bars while the investigation proceeded, and they still could not communicate with their lawyers.

Rumours still flew thick and fast. Dullman might have been the leader of the dynamite gang, people said, but whom was he working for? Although a few Canadians still suspected Boer sympathizers, public attention focused on people who feared Buffalo's loss of prestige as a major Great Lakes port, and – thanks to John Murray's remark – the Fenians. The Toronto *Globe* stated:

"Violent articles in inflammable American newspapers have, it is thought, stirred some of the more bitter enemies of Britain to a deed of desperation calculated to destroy hundreds of human lives and to utterly ruin property valued at millions of dollars. Canada is regarded as the special stomping ground for insidious attacks of such a nature, and nothing would be more natural than that ignorant or reckless characters might have been prompted to an effort to make this country do penance to suit fire-eating Anglophobes on the other side of the line."

The *Globe* editor also commented somewhat self-righteously on what he perceived to be differing Canadian and American attitudes toward the concepts of law and justice.

"All persons [in Canada] unite in condemning in the strongest possible terms the outrage and everyone connected with it. But there has not been the slightest manifestation toward the suspected trio. They occasioned emphatic comment whenever they were brought to the public gaze, but the populace made no demonstration. This is a subject of favorable contrast to the reception which such outrages invite in other portions of this enlightened continent. People are asking, 'What would have been done to three Canadians if they should attempt to blow up the Erie Canal in New York State?' The consensus of the answers is that the perpetrators would never live to realize what arrest for such a crime would mean."

Engineers who examined the damaged locks reported that, in their opinion, the act of sabotage had been clumsy. They would have the lock back in operation in time for the opening of the navigation season, at a trifling cost of about $5,000. They added that if the dynamite charges had been expertly placed, the result would have been disastrous. If the gates had been blown off, Thorold and Merritton would have been inundated. Water would have swept across low-lying flats strewn with cottages, mills, and factories. Roads and the railway would have been swamped, and the canal would have been out of operation for months. The engineers speculated that the destruction of property and loss of life would have been comparable to that of the catastrophic Johnstown Flood of Pennsylvania which occurred in 1889 when a dam burst.

Meanwhile, the prisoners were kept in jail under heavy guard. There was still concern that friends from the United States would attempt to break them out. Inspector Murray and Detective Mains crossed the border to enquire about the movements of the three men when they were in Buffalo. Dullman had claimed that he didn't know Walsh and Nolan, but informants in Buffalo said the three were often seen together and that they always seemed to have a lot of money. The Chief of Police in Buffalo told Murray the suspects were strangers in his city. He had learned that Nolan and Walsh had moved from one hotel to another and had given their address as Dublin, Ireland. A "special telegraphic report" from the State Department in Washington D.C. said that an inquiry had been made that completely exonerated the Buffalo grain handlers from all connections with the crime. The report laid the blame on "Irish Secret Associations."

On April 26, an officer from the Canadian Army's Stanley Barracks in Toronto arrived with soldiers to replace the special constables guarding key points on the canal. Inspector Murray showed up at the Welland jail with a photographer to take mug shots of the suspects. Walsh and Nolan were photographed without any problem. However, Dullman made a sudden rush at the camera and threw it down, smashing it to pieces. Murray jumped on him, and subdued him with the help of three other men.

The jailer put Dullman in irons. Another camera was brought in, and Dullman had his picture taken at gunpoint. He sullenly remarked that he might as well be dead as where he was.

Murray told the press that, while there was still a lot of investigative work to be done, he was certain that he would be able to gather enough evidence to have all three suspects convicted and sent to prison for a long time. His main concern was that one of the trio would turn Queen's evidence. That was a form of plea-bargaining of which Murray disapproved. He believed he could get to the bottom of things without any of the suspects agreeing to testify against the others in return for a lighter sentence.

On April 30, the day of the preliminary trial, the little town of Welland resembled an armed camp. Red-coated soldiers in white helmets, with bayonets fixed on their rifles, surrounded the courthouse. Others patrolled the main street and a five-mile stretch of the canal. Excitement over the trial had brought crowds of strangers to town. The little courtroom was packed, and a squad of soldiers stood between the prisoners and the spectators.

The three accused were seated together, but Dullman seemed to make every attempt to disassociate himself from the other two, even pulling his chair slightly away from them. Nolan and Walsh, still represented by McBurney, often whispered to each other and to their counsellor. Dullman sat quietly, not even speaking to his lawyer, W.M. German, a member of provincial parliament who had replaced Mr. Crow. It was as though Dullman was pretending that only Walsh and Nolan were on trial and he was merely an observer.

All three men entered pleas of not guilty. Magistrate Logan heard evidence from eighteen witnesses that directly implicated Walsh and Nolan in the bombing. The testimony strongly, but not conclusively, pointed to Dullman as an active member of the conspiracy. Two American officers, Sergeant John Malone of the Niagara Falls, New York, Police Department, and Customs Agent Charles Lewis, told the court that they had shadowed the three as suspected drug smugglers, and there was no doubt that Dullman was well-acquainted with Nolan and Walsh. The prisoners were committed to stand trial at the Spring Assize Court, scheduled to open on May 22.

John Murray took advantage of the time to go to the United States to dig up information on the suspects. Murray was a meticulous investigator who sought out evidence like a bloodhound. He travelled from one American city to another, interviewing people, following clues, and looking into new leads. He arrived back in Toronto on May 17, and even though the trial was due to begin in four days, he gave the *Globe* a full account of what he had learned.

In the spring of 1894, John Nolan and another Irishman named John Marna arrived in New York from Liverpool, England. Nolan found work as a machinist in Philadelphia, and Marna was employed as a bartender in Washington D.C. The men corresponded with each other, as well as with fellow Irish immigrants. On a trip home to Ireland in 1896, Nolan and Marna met John Walsh. He accompanied them when they sailed back to the United States.

LIFE IMPRISONMENT.

Welland Canal Dynamiters Get the Limit of the Law.

Jury Returns a Verdict of Guilty After a Brief Consideration of the Evidence—Excellent Case Presented by the Crown—No Evidence on Behalf of Nolan and Walsh, and Very Little on Behalf of Dullman—Mr. Johnston's Brilliant and Clever Address to the Jury—Chancellor Boyd's Comments on the Case—The Prisoners Made No Plea—A Globe Reporter Visits Them After Sentence—Dullman Expresses His Disappointment.

Toronto Globe of John Nolan (top) Karl Dullman and John Walsh, the Welland Canal Dynamiters.

Sometime in late 1896 or early 1897, Nolan, Marna, and Walsh went to New York and joined an organization called the Napper Tandy Club. Members met in a hall at the corner of 16th Street and Third Avenue. To the public eye, the club was a benevolent social group that assisted needy Irish immigrants. It was really the local branch of the secretive *Clan-na-Gael* Society (Society of Gaelic Families).

After the failure of the Fenians, Irish Americans who considered themselves Irish patriots founded *Clan-na-Gael* in 1869. Its goal was the same: the liberation of Ireland by means of violent acts against Great Britain. By 1896, *Clan-na-Gael* had a membership of more than 10,000, all of whom paid dues toward the great cause. It had been responsible for several bombings in London, and twenty-nine known members had been extradited from the United States to Britain to be tried for involvement in what today would be called terrorist activities.

Marna's involvement with *Clan-na-Gael* ended abruptly. On March 12, 1900, he was found dead in his rooming house in Washington D.C., shot through the heart. An inquest found no evidence of foul play and returned a verdict of suicide. However, no one had any explanation as to why Marna would take his own life. As a Roman Catholic, he would have believed that suicide meant eternal damnation. Moreover, in most suicide cases where a firearm is involved, the fatal wound is in the head.

One month after Marna's suspicious death, Nolan and Walsh received instructions through the Napper Tandy Club to go to Philadelphia. They were to travel under false names. At Reading Depot, they were met by a man whom Murray was sure belonged to *Clan-*

na-Gael's inner circle and was known within the Society as Number One. This mysterious individual, whose identity was still unknown to the police, was believed to have been involved in anti-British activities for over twenty years.

The stranger gave Nolan and Walsh a hundred dollars in cash and two railway tickets to Buffalo. He told them that in Buffalo they were to go to the Stafford House where they would meet Karl Dullman, a man previously unknown to them. They were to do whatever he told them and ask no questions.

Nolan and Walsh followed instructions and met Dullman at the Stafford House, where he had been waiting for two or three days. The three spent a lot of time talking in Nolan and Walsh's room, where they also did a good bit of drinking. A day or so after their initial meeting, the three checked out of the Stafford House and began a routine of moving from hotel to hotel. Nolan and Walsh were once seen leaving Dullman's room carrying satchels called telegraph grips. According to Murray's information, the dynamite in the satchels was in the shape of cakes. Soon after, people in Thorold began to notice strangers hanging around the canal. After the bombing, Walsh and Nolan were to have met Dullman in Buffalo to get paid for their work.

In his detailed account, Murray named people Nolan and Walsh had met since their arrival in New York six years earlier. He knew where the two men had worked and the addresses at which they had resided. He had spoken to former employers, members of hotel staffs, and quite likely underworld characters who might have information on such details as cakes of dynamite hidden in telegraph grips. Murray's notebook was probably filled with scraps of conversation passed onto him by waiters, bellhops, and maids who couldn't help but overhear men who'd had a drink or two too many. Inspector John Murray was *very* thorough. Today, his sharing of so much information with the press on the eve of an important trial might be seen as arrogant or foolish, but it wasn't unusual for the time.

The prisoners were in court on May 22, but the trial was delayed for two days because Nolan and Walsh were without counsel. German was there for Dullman, but McBurney was no longer representing the other two. It seemed that whoever was providing the money for the defence had decided that Nolan and Walsh were lost causes and not worth the expense. The trial finally got under way on May 24, before Chancellor Sir John Alexander Boyd. Prosecuting for the crown was Ebenezer F.B. Johnston, one of the most formidable attorneys in Ontario. A local lawyer named G.R. Burson had been appointed to represent Nolan and Walsh.

There was little doubt as to the outcome of the trial as far as Nolan and Walsh were concerned. Witness after witness took the stand and identified them as the men who had planted the dynamite. Inspector Murray's evidence connected them with the Napper Tandy Club and *Clan-na-Gael*. Police had found dynamite fuses in their hotel room.

However, the case against Dullman wasn't so open-and-shut. Although he had clearly been associated with Nolan and Walsh, that didn't necessarily mean he had been involved in the plot. But the circumstantial evidence was strong. Of particular interest was the testimony of one witness who swore that he had overheard a conversation in which Walsh had told Dullman, "Nolan must be kept sober, or it will be impossible to pull off the job."

The trial lasted two days. Thirty-three witnesses were questioned and cross-examined, and some 60,000 words of evidence were taken down. At 6:05 pm on May 25, the jury retired. Thirty-five minutes later, they returned with a verdict of guilty for all three prisoners.

For what he termed "a crime against civilization", Chancellor Boyd sentenced each of the accused to life imprisonment in the Kingston Penitentiary. He said that Walsh and Nolan were pawns who would do anything for "filthy lucre", but that Dullman, the leader, was the worst of the lot because he acted purely out of hatred. Nolan and Walsh had nothing to say and showed no emotion as sentence was passed. Dullman went pale and muttered, "That's a just judge."

Later, a *Globe* reporter interviewed the convicted men individually in their jail cells. Walsh laughed at the idea of a life sentence, and said, "I'm glad His Honour didn't make it a day longer."

Then he spoke longingly of his home in Dublin and wept for the wife and children he had left behind. He admitted that Dullman was the leader and a man to be protected "at all sacrifice." His closing words to the reporter were, "I'll have to be a British subject now. Good night, your honour, and thank you for calling, but I'm sorry that it wasn't hanging that I got."

Nolan told the reporter that he wouldn't whimper over his sentence, but it angered him that he'd been portrayed as a man who would commit a villainous act for pay. He was indignant that the court hadn't been more lenient with Dullman. Nolan said that if he'd been given the chance to testify, he would have committed perjury, no matter what the cost to himself, if it would have protected Dullman. "I knew we were in for it," he said, "but they had no case against Dullman."

The reporter found Dullman to be the most bitter of the three. He said he had been convicted on lies, especially the testimony concerning his alleged conversation with Walsh about Nolan's lack of sobriety. "Do you suppose that if I were a conspirator, I would allow anyone within three feet of me while I was speaking on a matter of that kind?"

Dullman also told the reporter that he had confessed to German that Karl Dullman wasn't his real name. The lawyer had told him that the magistrate might give him a light sentence if he would tell the whole truth about who he was and whom he'd been working for. But Dullman had insisted that he couldn't give up his secrets. "I have no doubt I will become acclimatized to the place they call Kingston," he said. "I have refused to disclose my identity, and I will continue in that course, although I will die in a place like this."

None of the convicted men would tell the police anything about the mystery man who had met Walsh and Nolan in Philadelphia, or anything about *Clan-na-Gael*. They were put on a train for Kingston where iron bars and grim stone walls awaited them. But the public would soon hear about Karl Dullman and *Clan-na-Gael* again.

In 1889, Dr. Patrick Henry Cronin of Chicago, a high-ranking member of *Clan-na-Gael*, had been murdered. Members of a clique within the Society who called themselves Camp 20 had suspected him of embezzling *Clan-na-Gael* funds and of being a spy for the British government. Cronin's murder caused a bitter rift in *Clan-na-Gael*, dividing it into the Camp 20 faction and the Cronin faction.

One of the most prominent members of the Cronin side was Luke Dillon. Born to Irish parents in Leeds, England, he had grown up in New Jersey. As a young man, Dillon joined the U.S. Army and fought in the Indian wars in Montana and Wyoming. He eventually settled in Philadelphia, where he started out as a shoe maker and then went into banking. Dillon married and became the father of five children.

Dillon had a passionate love for Ireland, though he had never set foot there, and became one of *Clan-na-Gael's* most notorious agents. In 1884-1885, he was involved in the bombings of Scotland Yard, the Junior Carlton Club, and the British Parliament building. Those exploits earned him the nickname Dynamite Luke and legendary status among Irish nationalists in both Ireland and the United States.

But Dr. Cronin had been a close personal friend, and Dillon was determined to see his killers brought to justice. Forsaking *Clan-na-Gael's* oath of secrecy (to an extent), Dillon assisted police in tracking down the suspected assassins, one of whom was arrested in Winnipeg. His testimony in court helped send two of the killers to prison for life.

Dynamite Luke had remained an active member of *Clan-na-Gael*, the rift in the Society having been repaired after the demise of Camp 20. He had somehow managed to avoid being arrested and extradited for the London bombings. He'd kept a low profile, and not even that tenacious sleuth Inspector John Murray came across his name during his investigation of the Welland Canal bombing.

Then in March of 1902, the Buffalo *Express* revealed that Karl Dullman, one of the men serving life sentences in Canada's Kingston Penitentiary, was in fact Dynamite Luke Dillon! The photograph Dullman had so violently objected to being taken in the Welland jail had been compared to one taken of Luke Dillon during the Cronin murder trial. They were clearly photos of the same man. Just to be sure, American police showed the picture of Karl Dullman to several people who had known Luke Dillon. They all identified the man in the picture as Dynamite Luke.

The question was finally put to the prisoner, who had been registered into the Kingston Penitentiary as Karl Dullman. He'd been at hard labour for almost two years, breaking rocks in the prison yard. He'd had no visitors and had received no letters. In reply to the question, he said, "I am Luke," and nothing more.

In July 1914, thanks to good behaviour and petitions from Roman Catholic organizations, Dillon was released on parole and deported to the United States. He finally admitted that he and his confederates had dynamited the Welland Canal out of sympathy for the Boers. Dillon returned to his family, whom he hadn't seen since the spring of 1900. His wife and children hadn't known that he was in a prison in Canada and had thought he was dead.

John Walsh had already died in prison. John Nolan was released not long after Dillon because of failing health and died shortly after. Inspector John Wilson Murray was on a case when he died of a sudden stroke on June 12, 1906. Dynamite Luke Dillon, alias Karl Dullman, died in 1930 at the age of 81, still a loyal member of *Clan-na-Gael*.

Henry Wagner: Pirate of the Georgia Strait

Henry Wagner

Henry Wagner was one of those Wild West desperadoes who somehow was overlooked by the dime novelists and film makers who transformed bandits like Jesse James and killers like Billy the Kid into icons. In his time, Wagner was almost legendary. He was a gunman who participated in numerous robberies and shot it out with lawmen. His ability to evade the forces of law and order and his ethnic background, which was either Dutch or German, earned him the nickname "the Flying Dutchman," a dark inference to a ghostly ship that supposedly haunted the high seas. It was said that any sailor who saw the Flying Dutchman was doomed. Wagner's nickname was, therefore, appropriate because he had no qualms about killing anyone who got in his way.

Wagner was believed to have ridden with the Hole-in-the-Wall gang, the notorious outlaw band led by Robert Leroy Parker and Harry Longabaugh, alias Butch Cassidy and the Sundance Kid. Starting in 1887, and operating out of a secret hideout in the wilds of Wyoming, the Hole-in-the-Wall bandits were one of the last great outlaw gangs of the Old West. Their depredations drew the attention of lawmen, bounty hunters, and Pinkerton detectives. But it wasn't until the turn of the 20th century that the United States Cavalry moved against the outlaws and broke the gang's power.

Some of the bandits went down in blazing shootouts. Others were captured and packed off to prison. Butch Cassidy and the Sundance Kid fled to South America, where they were allegedly killed a few years later in a gun battle with Bolivian soldiers. But the Flying Dutchman, if he was indeed a member of the Hole-in-the-Wall gang, escaped its demise.

There is no known documentary evidence that Henry Wagner robbed banks and trains with Butch Cassidy and the Sundance Kid. But that doesn't mean there is no basis to the legend. Wagner went by at least a dozen aliases, including Harry Ferguson. And even though a few desperadoes like Ben Kilpatrick, Harvey Logan, and Bill Carver were known to make up the gang's core, at least a hundred drifters, rustlers, and unemployed cowboys were hangers-on or passing members.

What is known for certain is that in 1902, soon after the break-up of the Hole-in-the-Wall gang, Wagner was arrested in the state of Washington for the attempted murder of a sheriff. He was sentenced to fourteen years in the penitentiary at Walla Walla. Wagner was a difficult prisoner, often in trouble with the warders, and likely spent a lot of time in "the hole", a dark isolation dungeon found in almost every prison of that era, where convicts were kept on a diet of bread and water.

Wagner was released in 1911. He was now in his mid-forties, but he was still an unrepentant hard case and determined to pick up where he had left off. It didn't occur to him that the days were over when all an outlaw needed were nerves of steel, a fast gun, and a fast horse. Hard-riding bandits who had followed leaders like Jesse James and Butch Cassidy were in prison or Boot Hill .

But the outlaw trail was all Henry Wagner had ever known – or wanted to know. He teamed up with another ex-convict named Bill Julian. It was an unusual partnership. While six-foot-tall Wagner was the quintessential Wild West "bad guy", tough and of a violent nature, Julian was quiet and mild-mannered. But he was nonetheless a criminal who would rather steal than engage in honest labour. Like Wagner, he went by several aliases and had once escaped from a prison in Georgia.

Wagner and Julian went on a spree of armed robbery and burglary that took them through Washington, Idaho, and Oregon. On a couple of occasions, they were actually apprehended but then were released before their captors could discover who they were. The Flying Dutchman was once again living up to his nickname.

Then one night late in 1912, the spree came to an abrupt end. Wagner and Julian were burglarizing the post office in a small Washington community on Puget Sound when the postmaster interrupted them. Without hesitation, Wagner pulled his gun and shot the man dead.

The bandits fled empty-handed. It wasn't long before the murder was discovered and a sheriff's posse was hunting them. Knowing that railway stations would be watched and every road patrolled, Wagner realized the only chance of escape was by sea. Under cover of night, he and Julian stole a power boat named the *Spray* and disappeared into the mists of Puget Sound. They headed for Canadian waters, where they believed they would be beyond the reach of American law.

If Wagner had in fact ridden with the Hole-in-the-Wall gang, he might have been aware that other members had, from time to time, sought sanctuary in Canada. The Sundance Kid had dodged the law by riding into what is now Alberta. A lesser known outlaw, Canadian-born Sam Kelly, had maintained a hideout just north of the international border in present day Saskatchewan. It was the northern terminus of a network of outlaw way stations that stretched all the way to Mexico. After the gang's dissolution, some of the scattered outlaws joined rustler bands that drove stolen cattle and horses across the border from Montana and North Dakota into Canadian territory.

The Flying Dutchman was in a different situation from those outlaws who practically lived in the saddle. In fleeing from American law, he had come into possession of a high-powered boat. He found himself in territory that must have seemed like the answer to a desperado's prayer. It was a coastal wilderness of rugged, sparsely populated land and a maze of inlets, islands, and coves where a predator like him could hide between raids. Most inviting to Wagner, there didn't seem to be a very strong police presence -- no United States marshals, gun-toting sheriffs, or Pinkerton detectives -- just a few British Columbia police constables thinly spread across a region bigger than many American states.

Henry Wagner might not ever have driven a boat before he and Julian stole the *Spray*. But he was about to become something unique in the annals of Canadian crime: an Old West outlaw turned pirate. Generations after piracy had been suppressed on the high seas, the Flying Dutchman plundered the Georgia Strait like a reincarnated buccaneer.

The robberies began late in the winter of 1912 and continued into 1913. Up and down the east coast of Vancouver Island and the opposite mainland shore, a mysterious thief broke into homes and businesses in the night and carried off money and property. He came and went like a ghost, and the only evidence he left behind was the mark in the sand where he had beached his boat. Residents in communities all along the shore were talking about the "phantom prowler" and wondering where he would strike next.

In his headquarters at Nanaimo, Chief Constable David Stephenson of the British Columbia Provincial Police, the commanding law enforcement officer for that district of Vancouver Island, was wondering the same thing. He was aware that coastal residents were getting impatient with the failure of the BCPP to catch the marauder. He had been studying the locations and dates of the robberies, and he believed that they followed a cycle that seemed to focus on the town of Union Bay.

Situated near the Cumberland coal mines, Union Bay was a busy port with freighters and other vessels and watercraft constantly coming and going. Whoever the pirate was, his boat could certainly be inconspicuous in all that traffic and could go unnoticed at a dock in a crowded harbour. Union Bay had been hit more than once. The lone BCPP officer stationed there, Constable J. "Big Mack" McKenzie, had kept lonely vigils at night, patrolling the town and watching places he thought could be targets. But it seemed that the mysterious robber was spying on *him*, because the robberies always took place in a part of town far from where Big Mack's rounds had taken him.

Stephenson had a hunch that the pirate was due to pay another visit to Union Bay. The town's Fraser and Bishop General Store, which was not only a prosperous business, but also housed the local post office, had not yet been robbed. It presented a very tempting target, especially if the "phantom prowler" was confident that he could plunder it without interference from Constable McKenzie.

Stephenson didn't doubt McKenzie's efficiency as a policeman or his dedication to duty. Big Mack had proven himself an exemplary officer on numerous occasions, breaking up brawls among miners, and even single-handedly putting down a riot. But the rash of robberies called for extraordinary measures.

Stationing extra constables in Union Bay would only discourage the pirate and send him plundering somewhere else. Stephenson wanted to lay a trap. He called into his office two police recruits he'd been training, Harry Westaway and Gordon Ross.

Scottish-born Ross was a British Army veteran who had served in the South African War. He had immigrated to Canada and met Westaway, a native of Prince Edward Island. The two became friends. Sharing a love of adventure, they had travelled west and signed up with the BCPP.

Stephenson told the rookie policemen that he was sending them on a special assignment. He explained the situation in the Georgia Strait and his reasons for thinking the pirate would strike again at the Fraser and Bishop General Store in Union Bay. They were to pose as men looking for work. They were not to reveal to anybody, especially Constable McKenzie, that they were police officers. If they were seen speaking to Big Mack, the robber might be tipped off. Nobody but the Union Bay postmaster would know who they really were and why they were in town.

Westaway and Ross were enthusiastic about the assignment. They knew that Stephenson had given it to them only because the BCPP was undermanned and no constables with more experience were available. They saw this undercover job as their chance to prove themselves.

Late in April 1913, Westaway and Ross arrived in Port Union. They took a room in a hotel and then wandered around town enquiring about employment. Helpful local people told them jobs were scarce for the time being, but if they stuck around for a while, there was a chance of men being taken on at the coal mines and the docks. It was just what they wanted to hear. Now they had a legitimate reason for hanging around town.

Constable McKenzie had noted the appearance of the two strangers in town. Ever on the alert for potential robbery suspects, he questioned them briefly and made enquiries at their hotel and with people he'd seen speaking to them. Big Mack was satisfied that the newcomers were what they said they were, men who just wanted to find jobs. He didn't know that they had secretly met with the postmaster, who gave them a key to Fraser and Bishop General Store.

On their first night in Union Bay, Westaway and Ross slipped out of their hotel unseen and, just as stealthily, used the key to let themselves into the general store. They concealed themselves and began the long, tedious vigil in the dark, taking turns at grabbing a few hours of sleep. No phantom prowler came sneaking in through a jimmied door or window. Before daybreak, Ross and Westaway quietly left the store, locked the door behind them, and kept to the shadows as they returned to their hotel and crept back into their room.

The two officers repeated this routine the next night and several nights after that. No one tried to break into the general store. In the daylight hours, as they poked around town and chatted with the locals, they learned that other businesses had been burglarized. Was the pirate on to them, or was it coincidence? They didn't ask questions about those crimes. McKenzie would handle that. Stephenson's orders had been for them to stake out only the general store.

Ross and Westaway spent ten monotonous, chilly nights in the store. Nothing happened. They were probably entertaining doubts as to whether police work was really as exciting as it was cracked up to be and wondering if Stephenson had sent them on a wild goose chase. Then, on the night of March 4, the Chief Constable's hunch proved to be dead on.

As usual, Ross and Westaway waited until well after dark before leaving their hotel room to go to the general store for what they thought would be another long, boring night. As they approached the store, they realized something was wrong when they saw a brief flash of light in a window of the post office part of the building. It was only because, at closing

147

time, someone had forgotten to pull the blind all the way down for the night, that they saw that quick warning flash.

Ross and Westaway quietly entered the building through the post office door. It was dark inside, but enough thin light from outside filtered through the unshaded window for them to see that the door connecting the post office to the store was open. It should have been closed.

Westaway silently pulled down the blind so they wouldn't be silhouetted against the window. Then, with Ross in the lead, the two officers approached the door. From the main part of the store, they heard a floorboard creak. Ross saw another flash of light that lasted only a second. "Someone's here," he whispered. Westaway drew his service revolver, a gun that was so old, it was almost an antique. Ross's only weapon was his police billy club, and it was in his coat pocket. All he had in his hand was a flashlight.

Ross went through the door first and commanded, "Put up your hands or I'll shoot!" as he switched on the flashlight. The beam caught two men crouched beside a counter. One of them brandished a .44 calibre pistol. Instinctively, Ross hurled himself at the gunman. There was a sharp report, and flame from the muzzle momentarily lit the room like the flash of a camera bulb. Hot pain seared Ross's arm as the slug creased the skin. The shot didn't slow Ross's bull-like charge, but behind him Westaway crumpled to the floor with a bullet in his chest.

As Ross tackled the gunman before he could fire again, he shouted for Westaway to get the other man. He didn't realize that his partner had been shot, and the other man had bolted for the door. Abandoning his own partner, Bill Julian fled from the general store. He ran to the harbour and jumped into the *Spray*. To his surprise, he couldn't get the motor started. Henry Wagner trusted nobody -- not even his partner-in-crime. Wagner had removed a small but vital part from the motor, rendering it inoperable. Julian made his escape from Port Union in a small rowboat he and Wagner towed behind the *Spray* in case they needed extra space for their plunder.

In the Fraser and Bishop General Store, where miners bought their pit boots and chewing tobacco, mothers purchased flour and tea for their pantries, and children were treated to sticks of candy, Constable Gordon Ross was entangled in the fight of his life. Ross was as big as Henry Wagner, and he was an ex-soldier who had known war. But the Flying Dutchman was a hard-bitten veteran of brawling outlaw camps where only the toughest survived. A clash on a battlefield was nothing at all like a deadly hand-to-hand struggle.

Ross had dropped his flashlight, which broke when it hit the floor, leaving the combatants in darkness. Wagner still had the gun in his hand but couldn't bring it to bear for a direct shot as he and Ross grappled, knocking over shelves and barrels. Wagner's finger was on the trigger while his gun hand was twisted this way and that, and the weapon discharged repeatedly until it was empty. A couple of the muzzle flashes had been close enough to burn Ross's skin, but the bullets passed harmlessly through his clothing.

Ross grabbed Wagner by the throat, but the powerful outlaw broke free from his grip. Ross went for the throat again, only to feel a jolt of pain as Wagner bit hard on two of his fingers. Wagner then began to pistol whip Ross with the empty gun. While blows fell on his head and shoulders, Ross managed to pull his billy from his pocket.

By now the two men were on the floor, rolling and thrashing in blood. Wagner continued to strike Ross with the gun, and Ross gave back as good as he got with the billy. Then a solid blow to the head stunned Wagner and he dropped the gun. Ross took advantage of the moment and delivered a couple of hard cracks to the Flying Dutchman's head, knocking him out cold.

Wagner lay still, but Ross was barely conscious himself. His head was lacerated and he was bleeding. Ross handcuffed the pirate, then crawled over to where Westaway lay. Westaway had dragged himself under a table. When Ross reached him, the young constable whispered, "Goodbye, Gordon," and died.

It seemed to Ross that no one in Port Union had heard the racket of the fight or even the gunshots. Ross could barely hold his head up. He was afraid of what might happen if he passed out, and the outlaw regained consciousness. In desperation, he threw his billy club at the window in the front door.

Minutes earlier, Constable McKenzie had been patrolling in another part of town when he heard what he was sure were gunshots. He hurried in the direction of the sounds, but because they'd been muffled, he couldn't pinpoint the precise source. Then, as he approached the general store, he heard the unmistakable noise of breaking glass.

Big Mack ran to the front door of Fraser and Bishop's and broke it open with his shoulder. As he burst in he shouted a warning to whoever was in there that he had a gun – which he didn't. He shone his flashlight and saw what looked like a scene from a war zone. The interior of the store was a shambles, with fallen shelves, broken crockery, and scattered merchandise. A man with a revolver in his hand lay motionless in a pool of blood under a table. In the midst of the debris on the floor was another gun. A man with cuffs on his wrists lay prone, a few moans coming from his bloodied lips. On his knees, looking up at McKenzie, was a man with a battered face who gasped, "I'm a police officer."

After seeing Ross's badge, McKenzie lit a lamp and took a close look at Westaway. The front of his shirt was saturated with blood. An autopsy would show that Wagner's bullet had nicked Westaway's heart.

While Big Mack administered first aid from the store's pharmaceutical supplies, Ross explained what had happened. Another officer might have been indignant over being kept in the dark about a stakeout in his own town, but McKenzie saw the practical sense of it and wasn't a man much given to pettiness. More than anything, he was angry that a young officer had been murdered.

McKenzie didn't recognize the unconscious prisoner as anyone he had seen before. He searched the man and found a homemade device that accounted for the flashes of light Ross and Westaway had seen.

Wagner had a pair of dry cell batteries in his pants pocket. They were attached by wire to a switch and a small light bulb he could hold in his hand. It was an excellent tool for night time burglaries.

Wagner eventually came around. He was groggy and in pain, but alert enough to be surly and uncooperative. He refused to identify himself or answer any questions. The following day, after Ross had grabbed a few hours of badly needed sleep, Ross and McKenzie took the prisoner to Nanaimo.

In police headquarters, Chief Constable Stephenson took a long, hard look at the captive and then consulted his stack of wanted posters. A mole on the prisoner's cheek, along with other physical features, identified him as Henry Wagner, formerly an inmate of the Walla Walla penitentiary and now wanted in the state of Washington for the murder of a postmaster.

The name Henry Wagner caught the attention of all three officers. Who hadn't heard of the notorious outlaw who had blazed his way across the American West? So *he* was the elusive pirate of the Georgia Strait! Stephenson told Ross that he had captured none other than the infamous Flying Dutchman. But the only thing that mattered to Ross was that the man who had shot his friend would stand trial for murder.

His identity revealed, the prisoner admitted that he was Henry Wagner. When asked who his accomplice was, he didn't hesitate to name Bill Julian. As far as Wagner was concerned, Julian was a coward who had run out on him when he should have stayed to fight. The two of them could have taken care of Ross and then made their getaway.

A BCPP constable named George Hannay saw Wagner in the Nanaimo jail and said that he was certain he had seen the prisoner and another man on Lasqueti Island, which lay in the Georgia Strait northeast of Port Union and close to the mainland. There was an old abandoned cabin on it that the outlaws could have been using as a base. The police were sure that Julian was the man Hannay had seen with Wagner and that there was a good chance he was still hiding out on the island.

Hannay took a police party out to a small, rocky islet just off Lasqueti Island and within sight of the cabin. There was no sign of the fugitive, so they lay in wait for a few days. At last they saw Julian rowing toward Lasqueti in a small boat. Julian didn't resist when Hannay arrested him. The constables searched the cabin and the island and found most of the stolen property.

Now it was Bill Julian's turn to betray his partner. Julian had not fired the shot that killed Westaway, but under Canadian law, he was an accomplice in a crime that had resulted in murder and, therefore, was just as responsible as the man who had pulled the trigger. To escape accompanying Wagner to the gallows, Julian agreed to turn King's evidence. He talked to the police about what had happened in the general store the night Westaway was killed, provided detailed information about the many robberies, and agreed to testify for the Crown.

Wagner was tried for murder at the Spring Assizes in Nanaimo before Justice Morrison. Among the spectators in the courtroom was a United States Marshal who was prepared to take the Flying Dutchman into custody in the event of an acquittal. But there wasn't much chance of that. The testimonies of Gordon Ross and Bill Julian sealed his fate. Wagner was found guilty and condemned to death. Julian was sentenced to five years in prison for robbery. He was relieved to have escaped a meeting with the hangman, but he was fearful that Wagner might somehow get away and seek revenge. In court, the Flying Dutchman had promised he would do just that.

After his release from Walla Walla, Wagner had sworn that he would never again be captured alive. Constable Ross had given the lie to that boast. Now Wagner said that he would never hang. In spite of a close watch kept on him, Wagner attempted several times to commit suicide. He tried to strangle himself, he slashed his wrists, and he tried to bash his brains out against a brick wall. He assaulted guards in the hope that one would shoot him. All of his attempts to cheat the hangman failed.

Wagner was not permitted to have shaves or haircuts in case he might try to get hold of a razor or scissors. By August 28, the scheduled day of his execution, his hair and beard were long and scraggly. He'd had a "fit" the night before, but by pre-dawn had composed himself enough to have a breakfast of toast and coffee. Then he went to his death with a show of bravado worthy of an old-time pirate.

When Wagner was taken out to the jail yard where Arthur Ellis, Canada's official hangman, waited on the gallows, he suddenly ran up the steps to the scaffold and stood beneath the dangling rope. A surprised Mr. Ellis pulled the black cap over Wagner's head, fitted the noose around his neck, and sprang the trap door just as the attending clergyman began reciting the Lord's Prayer. Whatever the

Flying Dutchman's legend might have been in the American West, his execution set a record as the quickest hanging in Canadian history.

Old Creepy: The Saga of Alvin Karpis

Alvin Karpis

      With the exception of the Old West of Billy the Kid, Frank and Jesse James, and Butch Cassidy's Wild Bunch, no period of outlawry in North America has been more romanticized than the early years of the Great Depression. These were the "Dirty Thirties"

when the 1929 collapse of a poorly regulated stock market shut down factories and threw millions of people out of work. Banks foreclosed on the mortgages of homes and farms. Soup kitchens and breadlines became facts of life for destitute people. Desperation led to an increase in the crime rate. Much of that was due to small-time theft: shoplifting, burglary, mugging, and two-bit stick-ups, as unemployed men tried to steal what they could no longer get through honest labour.

However, most of the individuals whose criminal exploits earned them international notoriety were not "driven to it" by the social injustices of "hard times". Almost all of them had criminal records before the disastrous stock market crash. Some had served apprenticeships in crime by working for bootleggers during the Prohibition era of the Roaring Twenties. Others had been armed robbers, hijackers, and the paid thugs of big city crime bosses.

The arrival of the automobile had revolutionized crime. Fast cars and an ever-expanding network of roads and paved highways opened the way for the "automobile bandits", desperadoes who would swoop down on a small town bank, loot it at gunpoint, and then make a quick escape in a stolen car. The media of the time made celebrities of some of these criminals. Their brazen robberies and colourful nicknames sold newspapers. Some even achieved "Robin Hood" folk hero status among the poor and disposessed because they preyed on the hated banks and were hunted by the police, who were often resented as the strong arm of the rich and powerful.

Only a handful of these hoodlums became icons of Depression Era crime: Clyde Barrow and his girlfriend Bonnie Parker, George "Machine Gun" Kelly, Charles "Pretty Boy" Floyd, Lester Gillis – better known as Baby Face Nelson, and John Dillinger, the first of this bunch to be listed as Public Enemy Number One. Also in this rogues' gallery were Freddie and Arthur "Doc" Barker and their pal Alvin Karpis.

While all of the other headline-making outlaws were American born-and-bred, Karpis was Canadian. He was born in Montreal in 1907 to John and Anna Karpowicz, Lithuanian immigrants who named him Albin Francis. While Albin was still very young, his family moved to Topeka, Kansas, where he and his three sisters grew up. An elementary school teacher found his foreign-sounding name too awkward to pronounce, so she called him Alvin Karpis.

John Karpowicz worked hard at whatever jobs he took on, but the family was always poor. The fact that his father "worked like a slave" for little financial return left a strong impression on young Karpis. John was also a very strict father who administered discipline with a whip.

Karpis fell in with bad company early in life. While other boys were playing baseball, fishing, and making pocket money selling newspapers, Alvin was hanging out in the part of town that was on "the wrong side of the tracks." He found that he could earn a few dollars running errands for the prostitutes, pimps, and shady characters who inhabited the brothels, bars, and gambling dens. At the age of ten, Karpis made friends with an eighteen-year-old youth who had just been released from reformatory. One night the two of them broke into a grocery store and looted it of cash and merchandise. Karpis was hooked by the lure of easy money.

Karpis became an incorrigible juvenile delinquent. He learned to fight and how to case the stores he wanted to rob. He watched police officers walk their beats and became familiar with their routines. If he saw something he wanted in a shop window, he waited for just the right time at night to smash the window with a brick, grab the goods, and be gone before a cop could arrive. He was never caught.

When Karpis was fifteen, his family moved to Chicago where John got a job as a janitor. Alvin "went straight" for almost two years, employed as an errand boy and a shipping clerk. Then a doctor told him he had a weak heart and advised him to find less strenuous work. Honest labour had never appealed to Karpis anyway. He left home and went back to Topeka where he became involved in bootlegging and burglary.

Like many other footloose young men, Karpis hoboed around the country, hopping freight trains. But while many hoboes were honest men in search of work who couldn't afford to pay passenger fare, Karpis was a wanderer who kept a sharp eye for businesses that would be good targets for robbery. Karpis's first arrest occurred when "bulls" (railroad police) caught him riding on the roof of a boxcar in Florida. It was a minor offense that cost him thirty days in jail, but it gave him a criminal record that would soon have dramatic consequences.

In 1926 police caught Karpis burglarizing a warehouse in a small Kansas town. When the judge learned that the eighteen-year-old standing before him had been in jail previously, he decided to throw the book at him. He sentenced Karpis to five to ten years in the reformatory in Hutchinson, Kansas.

Like most prisons of the time, the Hutchinson reformatory was a place of punishment that offered little in the way of rehabilitation or reform. The food was bad, the prisoners' bunks crawled with vermin, and the slightest infraction of the rules landed an inmate in the "hole" – solitary confinement. Years later, Karpis recalled that he spent a lot of time in the hole, but he looked on his stint in Hutchinson as an opportunity to learn the ropes from more experienced criminals.

One of the many inmates Karpis befriended in Hutchinson was Lawrence Devol, a man in his mid-twenties who was a career criminal, exactly what Karpis aspired to be. As a bank burglar who was an expert at blowing safes with nitroglycerine, Devol was at the top of the prison hierarchy. Karpis looked up to him and considered himself fortunate to occupy a cell next to Devol's. During the long nights, he would listen for hours while this criminal mentor told him the tricks of the trade.

By the spring of 1929, Karpis and Devol had decided they'd had enough of Hutchinson. They cut through bars with hacksaws smuggled out of the workshop and escaped. The two fugitives travelled across the American West, stealing clothes, cars, guns, money, and anything else they needed. Karpis later recalled, "Being free again was wonderful."

Karpis and Devol pulled a few penny-ante stick-ups of small stores in Oklahoma, and then headed for Chicago with dreams of bigger, more lucrative heists. Devol ran into bad luck when police there recognized him. He was arrested and sent back to Hutchinson.

Karpis had enjoyed travelling and robbing with Devol, whom he considered "a cool character." Now he was alone and on the run. With nowhere else to turn, Karpis went home. It wasn't a pleasant experience for him.

Alvin had become the "black sheep" of the Karpowicz family. Having a convicted criminal in the fold bore a social stigma that touched everyone connected with the transgressor, especially parents and siblings. It wasn't unusual for the family of a criminal or "jailbird" to move away to a place where they weren't known. John wanted his wayward son to give himself up, serve his sentence, and then come back to his family and start over with a clean slate. "What you're doing is no good," he told Alvin repeatedly. "You'll be a wanted man all your life if you don't straighten out."

Karpis had no intention of turning himself in, but to his parents' delight he got a job at a local bakery. He wasn't wanted for any crime in Illinois, so the Chicago police weren't looking for him. For a little while, it appeared that Karpis was ready to settle down. Then the owner of the bakery ran into financial difficulties because of the stock market crash and laid him off. Karpis wasn't sorry about losing his job. "I was getting restless again. I spun out of Chicago, stealing and robbing."

Karpis was still a small-time hoodlum who worked alone or formed temporary partnerships with a succession of other petty crooks. He stole cars, stuck up gas stations, and burglarized pharmacies for narcotics that he sold to addicts. He still had ambitions of becoming a big-time gangster but felt that he was going nowhere. Then in 1930, he hooked up again with Lawrence Devol.

After being sent back to Hutchinson, Devol had requested a transfer to the prison at Lansing, Kansas, where inmates worked in a coal mine. The work was hard, dirty, and dangerous, but a convict who laboured like one of the mules that hauled the coal cars could have a lot of time knocked off his sentence. The more coal a man dug, the sooner he'd get out. After a few brutal months slaving in the bowels of the earth, Devol had been paroled.

Like Karpis, Devol had no intention of going straight. He had plans for himself and his young protégé, but first he wanted to do a favour for his buddies back in Lansing. Prison administrations were often corrupt, and funds that were supposed to provide for the basic needs of inmates were diverted into private pockets. One of the results of embezzlement in Lansing was a lack of replacements for inmates' worn-out clothing and shoes.

Devol and Karpis broke into a clothing store and swept the racks of shirts, pants, and shoes. They wrapped the goods up in packages addressed to inmates in Lansing and put them in the mail. None of the parcels had a return address, but the grateful recipients soon learned through the underworld grapevine who their benefactors were. Karpis thought the clothing caper was "a hell of a lark." It would soon prove to be more than that.

Having done their good deed for Devol's pals, the pair pulled a string of burglaries in Oklahoma, Kansas, and Missouri. The swag was always small, just enough money to tide them over until their next job. Meanwhile, Karpis learned something about Devol that was "beginning to shake me up a little."

In Perry, Oklahoma, Devol shot and killed a man who had the bad luck to stumble upon a burglary in progress. Not long after, in Lexington, Missouri, Devol got into a shootout with a police officer and killed him. Karpis later claimed that he wasn't with Devol on either occasion, and he was never implicated in those murders. But he said that when Devol described the killings to him, he had a gleam in his eyes that Karpis found troubling. His principal concern wasn't that Devol was trigger-happy and boasted about gunning men down. What worried Karpis was that he was now partners with a cop killer who would be sought by police everywhere. Karpis wondered if it might be smart for him to end his partnership with Devol. But Karpis had a strong sense of loyalty toward his criminal companions that would surface throughout his lawless career. "I didn't desert him," he wrote years later.

About the end of March, 1930, Devol and Karpis were driving through Kansas City in a stolen car when they were pulled over by two motorcycle cops. They gave the officers false names and tried to brazen it out, but the policemen found burglar tools in the car. The suspects were taken to the police station where, according to Karpis, "the Kansas City police beat the hell out of us." At that time, police interrogations often involved the "third degree" – beatings!

Hard cases that they were, Devol and Karpis wouldn't admit to anything. For Karpis, the rough stuff ended when a detective recognized him as an escapee from the Hutchinson reformatory. He had no option but to admit that he was Alvin Karpis. Still a two-bit punk in the eyes of the police, Karpis was packed off to his old jail.

Karpis had time added to his sentence for escaping custody, but he hadn't been connected to any of the crimes he had committed since breaking out. Investigators still didn't know that his partner Devol had killed the policeman in Lexington. Karpis saw his return to Hutchinson as a mere setback to his ambition to make big money as a professional criminal.

Karpis arrived back in Hutchinson with a deep hatred for cops. His ears were black from bruising and his upper body was "every colour of the rainbow." The prison doctor told him he'd probably lose his front teeth. The fact that he'd endured a savage beating from the police without cracking gained him the respect of other inmates. Even some of the guards grudgingly acknowledged that he was one tough customer.

Karpis got out of Hutchinson the same way Devol had. He requested a transfer to Lansing, where he could shorten his prison time by working in the coal mine. Karpis found the mine a wretched place, not only because of the back-breaking labour, but also because of the mules that bit and kicked, and the flying cockroaches that swarmed over the rations of bread dipped in syrup the men were given. Nonetheless, Karpis said later that, for him, Lansing was a "gold mine".

The Barkers

Other convicts quickly befriended Karpis because of the "lark" with the clothing and shoes. One was a short, sandy-haired man with a mouthful of gold teeth. One evening he stopped Karpis at the door of the mess hall, shook his hand and said, "I'm Freddie Barker. I already know who you are. Let's go in to supper together." When Karpis accepted the invitation, he took a major step toward the big money and notoriety he craved.

Twenty-seven-year-old Freddie was the youngest son of George Barker, an Ozark Mountains farmer and miner, and his wife Arizona Donnie, neè Clark. She was known to friends as "Arrie" and "Kate" but would one day enter outlaw legend as "Ma Barker".

Freddie and his older brothers, Herman, Lloyd, and Arthur ("Doc"), grew up in the isolated hill country of Missouri. George was shiftless, so the family was dirt poor. The boys received little schooling and were functionally illiterate. Their hero was the outlaw Jesse

James, and they emulated him by stealing and generally running wild. If neighbours complained to George about his sons' thieving or rowdiness, he would shrug his shoulders and say, "You'll have to talk to Mother. She handles the boys."

As far as Ma was concerned, her boys could do no wrong. People who accused them of theft and bad behaviour were all liars! If the police came calling, Ma wailed that they were persecuting the Barkers just because they were poor.

As the family moved around Missouri and Oklahoma, the Barker boys matured into hardened criminals. They were car thieves, burglars, and armed robbers. All wound up in prison at one time or another. Herman was an escapee, wanted for the murder of a policeman in Wyoming, when he got into a gunfight with police in Witchita, Kansas, on August 29, 1927. He killed another officer but was badly wounded and committed suicide rather than be taken alive.

Lloyd's criminal career ended in 1922 when he was sentenced to twenty-five years in the federal penitentiary in Leavenworth, Kansas, for mail robbery. He would be paroled in 1938 and go straight for the rest of his life. But he, too, would die violently, murdered by his wife in Colorado in 1949.

At the time he met Alvin Karpis in Lansing, Freddie was serving a sentence of five to ten years for burglary and grand larceny. He had a scar from a bullet wound inflicted during a gun battle with police a few years earlier. In the company the Barkers and Karpis ran with, such a scar was the equal of a war medal. Doc Barker, meanwhile, was in the state prison in McAlester, Oklahoma, where he was doing a life term for the murder of a night watchman in 1922.

Just as he had done with Devol, Karpis looked up to Freddie Barker. He thought of him as a tough, experienced professional who could teach him a lot. Freddie even knew how to get luxuries like canned chicken and fresh bread smuggled into his cell, and he shared them with his friends. Alvin and Freddie agreed that, when they got out of Lansing, they would form a partnership.

Barker was paroled in March, 1931, and Karpis the following May. Karpis had sped up his release by literally buying time from other convicts. Men who were in for life couldn't take advantage of the early release system, so they would allow other prisoners to claim some of the coal they'd dug in exchange for money. Karpis evidently had cash smuggled in to him.

Karpis and Barker met in Joplin, Missouri, where Ma resided. She had separated from George and was living with an alcoholic billboard painter named Arthur Dunlop. He was a poor provider, so Ma depended on her boys for support. With Herman dead and his brothers in jail, things had been pretty tough.

Freddie, Karpis, and a few of their hoodlum pals pulled a string of burglaries, all of them for "small potatoes". On May 22, police in Tulsa, Oklahoma, raided an apartment building and engaged in a gunfight with two suspects. There were no casualties, but the suspects escaped. Police much later concluded that they were Freddie Barker and Alvin Karpis, but not before June 10, when Freddie and Karpis were arrested. Karpis was jailed for a jewellery store burglary but got out after just three months because he returned the stolen goods. Barker was sent to Claremore, Oklahoma, to stand trial on another burglary charge but broke out of jail. The two hooked up again in Tulsa. Karpis said that he was tired of the small-time jobs and wanted to pull something big. Barker replied that he knew of a bank that would be easy to take.

On October 7, 1931, Alvin Karpis participated in his first armed bank robbery. Two ex-cons, Bill Weaver and Jimmie Wilson, were in on the job. In the dark hours of the morning, the gang broke into the Peoples Bank in the tiny community of Mountain View,

Missouri. Shortly before 9:00 a.m., two female employees entered the bank and found themselves facing masked men with guns in their hands. Karpis yelled, "Don't move! We're robbing this place." One of the women swooned, and Weaver caught her.

The robbers made the other woman open the vault. Karpis and Weaver scooped out the contents. Then they told the women to get inside and not come out for ten minutes. They closed the vault door without locking it, and hurried outside where Freddie was waiting at the wheel of the getaway car. As the gang sped out of town, they tossed two-inch roofing nails on the road to puncture the tires of any police cars that tried to follow them. When the bandits thought they'd put enough distance between themselves and Mountain View, they stopped to count the loot. They had $7,000 in cash and an equal amount in securities that could be fenced on the black market. Karpis was thrilled, and was anxious to hit a big bank. Barker felt that Karpis needed more experience before taking on a major heist.

The bandits headed for St. Paul, Minnesota. At that time, St. Paul was a "safe" town for criminals, thanks to a corrupt police department and a crime boss named Harry Sawyer who was the intermediary between the cops and the crooks. Bank robbers, kidnappers, bootleggers, and even killers could walk the streets and enjoy the pleasures of the speakeasies and brothels without fear of arrest, as long as they paid protection money and didn't commit any crimes within city limits. Anyone who pulled a robbery in St. Paul was fair game for the cops.

Barker and Karpis paid the obligatory visit to Sawyer, then rented an apartment. From this headquarters, they ranged across the state, pulling small-time burglaries and hold-ups, usually in the company of other thieves. They stripped warehouses and stores of anything that could be peddled on the black market and did an especially good business in stolen cigarettes. On two occasions, they pillaged entire small towns, taking the community's lone police officer hostage and then looting homes and businesses. Karpis would later have fond memories of these crimes, describing them the way another man might reminisce about events of a mischievous childhood. But there was nothing mischievous about a crime that occurred toward the end of 1931.

On the night of December 18, burglars broke into a clothing store in West Plains, Missouri. Witnesses spotted a 1931 DeSoto and took down the license plate number. The next day, the same car pulled into a West Plains garage to get two flat tires repaired. The suspicious garage owner phoned Sheriff C. Roy Kelly. When Kelly arrived at the garage, the occupants of the DeSoto immediately opened fire. The sheriff died with four bullets in his chest. The gunmen were later identified as Alvin Karpis, Freddie Barker, and Bill Weaver.

Speaking of the crime years later, Karpis would claim that only Barker and Weaver were in West Plains and that he had nothing to do with the tragedy. But Karpis was a confessed cop-hater, and at that time was at a point in his criminal career where he felt he still had to prove himself to older, more experienced thugs like Barker and Weaver. Crime historians examining the events of that day concluded that it was probably Karpis, armed with a .45 automatic pistol, who fired the shots that killed Sheriff Kelly, while a bullet from Barker's .38 revolver struck the officer's right arm. Alvin Karpis could now add murder to his criminal resume.

Clues led police investigating Kelly's slaying to a farm near Thayer, Missouri. The place was deserted but had obviously been chosen and equipped for defensive purposes. The house was on a hill with clear views in all directions. It was ringed by barbed wire, and the front gate was hooked up to an electronic alarm. The occupants had clearly left in a hurry. Inside the house, police found photographs of Karpis, Arthur Dunlop, and members of the Barker family, including Ma. There was a letter written to Ma from Lloyd in Leavenworth prison. Police also found a drawing of the interior of the First National Bank of West Plains.

Rewards were offered for the arrests of Fred Barker, Alvin Karpis, Arthur Dunlop, and "Old Lady Arrie Barker, Mother of Fred Barker." This was the first and probably only official notice concerning Ma Barker and any connection with the Barker gang before her death made newspaper headlines a few years later. It was also the first time Alvin Karpis had a price on his head.

Between hold-ups, Barker and Karpis resided in the security of St. Paul, paying Harry Sawyer a piece of the action. He saw to it that the police got their share of the stolen money, so no cops came pounding on Alvin and Freddie's apartment door. Sawyer's Green Lantern Saloon was a favourite outlaw hangout. It was there that Karpis and Barker mixed with a concentration of criminals that could be found nowhere else in America. Most of them would never be well known to anyone except law enforcement officers, but some were already infamous and others were on their way to national and even international notoriety.

Among them were Minneapolis gangster boss Isadore "Kid Cann" Blumenfeld, Al Capone gunman Gus Winkler, bank robbers Harvey Bailey and Frank "Jelly" Nash, and a bootlegger named George Barnes who would find his own dark corner in crime legend as "Machine Gun Kelly".

It was through this underworld socializing in St. Paul that the Barker-Karpis gang was formed in the dying days of 1931. The gang's membership would fluctuate considerably over the next few years, but Freddie Barker and Karpis emerged as the leaders. Only later would the false story circulate that Ma Barker led the gang.

Karpis got his wish to pull a major bank robbery on March 29, 1932, when the gang hit the North American Branch of the Northwestern National Bank in Minneapolis. In on the job with Karpis and Barker were two professional stick-up men named Tommy Holden and Phil Courtney, and Karpis's old pal Lawrence Devol, who had been paroled and was now on the run after killing three more police officers. The operation was well-planned.

Ma Barker

Holden waited in the getaway car in an alley behind the bank while the others burst in through the front door. Brandishing guns, they shouted orders at the staff and customers, warning them not to make a false move. Karpis and Courtney kept everyone covered while Barker and Devol forced the head cashier to open the safes in the big walk-in vault. It took them just a couple of minutes to fill the laundry bags they'd brought along.

Doc Barker

Then Devol looked out a front window and saw cops gathering on the street at both ends of the block. The police had somehow been alerted. The bandits hurried out through the back door to the alley, where they found Holden standing by the car, holding a detective at gunpoint. The detective was the only policeman who had thought to cover the back door, and Holden had taken him by surprise. Fortunately for the officer, Holden had only disarmed him.

The bandits piled into the car and roared out of the alley and down the street past the startled police officers. Nobody tried to stop them. Not a shot had been fired. No one had been hurt.

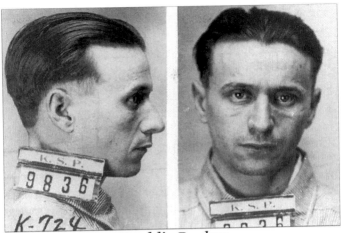
Freddie Barker

Back in their lair in St. Paul, the gang emptied the laundry bags and counted the loot. It was more money than Karpis had ever seen in his life: $75,000 in paper currency, $6,500 in coins, and $185,000 in bonds. The next day the robbery was headline news in American newspapers. Alvin Karpis had finally hit the big time.

Karpis and Freddie moved into another rented house in St. Paul with Ma and Arthur Dunlop. By this time, Alvin was practically a member of the Barker family. They weren't in the new residence for long when their landlady's son recognized Alvin and Freddie from photographs he had seen in a detective magazine. The accompanying article named them as suspects in the murder of Sheriff Kelly.

Alarmed that she might have killers as tenants, the landlady called the St. Paul police. Cops on Harry Sawyer's payroll held up the report through bureaucratic foot-dragging long enough for Karpis and Barker to be tipped off. When police raided the house on April 25, they found it abandoned.

The following morning, the naked body of Arthur Dunlop was discovered on the shore of Lake Fremstadt near Webster, Wisconsin. He had been shot three times at close range. The police suspected that Karpis and Freddie had murdered Dunlop because they thought he was an informer. And even if Dunlop wasn't a stool pigeon, he was nonetheless a liability. He was a drunk, and drunks had a tendency to talk too much. When Freddie decided that Dunlop had to go, Ma didn't protect her former lover from her homicidal son. Ma's boys knew what was best.

Ma, Freddie, and Karpis moved to Kansas City. Posing as a respectable family, Mrs. A.F. Hunter and sons, they rented an apartment. Neighbours thought Alvin and Freddie were successful insurance salesmen.

Alvin and Freddie soon hooked up with two escaped convicts, Francis Keating and

Harvey Bailey – later an accomplice of Machine Gun Kelly. Joining the gang were Jelly Nash, their old partners Devol and Holden, and a hoodlum named Bernard Phillips. Unbeknownst to the others, Phillips was a former crooked cop who had decided that robbing banks was more lucrative than taking bribes.

On June 17, this gang hit the Citizens National Bank in Fort Scott, Kansas, and got away with $47,000. That same day, an old Barker associate named Jess Doyle was released on parole from the Kansas state prison. He headed straight for Kansas City and joined the gang. The outlaws threw a lavish "coming out" party for him.

The good times were spoiled for this particular version of the Barker-Karpis gang just a few weeks later. On July 7, Kansas City police and a federal agent arrested Bailey, Holden, and Keating on a local golf course. Phillips, who was in the club house, escaped and warned the rest of the gang. Once again the police raided a suspect apartment, only to find the quarry gone.

Not until later did the gang learn that Phillips had once been a police officer. It didn't matter that he'd been a dirty cop. To Karpis and Barker, any connection to the law and authority was suspect. Bernard Phillips mysteriously disappeared and was believed to have been murdered.

Holden and Keating were sent back to prison in Leavenworth, but Bailey was held in Fort Scott to be tried for armed robbery because he had a bond from the Citizen's National Bank in his pocket. Karpis and Barker allegedly hired a shady lawyer named J. Earl Smith to defend him. Smith took the money they paid him, but he wasn't in court for Bailey's trial. A court-appointed lawyer was given the case, and Bailey was sentenced to a long prison term. He would soon escape.

Meanwhile, J. Earl Smith was lured by a mysterious phone call to a meeting with persons unknown. He was found shot to death. Alvin Karpis and Freddie Barker were high on the list of murder suspects.

In later years, Karpis would be evasive on the matter of murder. That is understandable considering that, when he collaborated with writers on his life story, he was a parolee who could face consequences if he admitted committing a homicide. He spoke of being involved in killings but wouldn't provide details. In his opinion, cops who got in the way of professional bank robbers going about their business were fair game. If a bandit shot a police officer, it was self-defence as far as Karpis was concerned.

Karpis admired Freddie's cold-blooded efficiency when it came to getting rid of anyone who double-crossed him or whom he considered a threat. However, whenever Karpis recalled an incident in which Freddie (or any other of his partners in crime) committed a murder, he always took care to say that he had not been present. One such case was that of Dr. Joseph P. Moran.

Doc Moran was a physician whose practice had been ruined by alcoholism. He had served a term in prison for performing illegal abortions. He had underworld connections and practiced out of a Chicago hotel room. Moran was more or less on call for criminals who couldn't very well go to hospital emergency rooms to have gunshot wounds treated. Among his specialties were fingerprint removal and the altering of facial features through a crude form of plastic surgery. Karpis and Barker knew of Moran by reputation and decided that if they didn't have fingerprints to leave at crime scenes, the police would have a harder time tracking them and gathering evidence against them. They made an appointment with Doc Moran.

For the hefty price of $500 each, Alvin and Freddie went through the painful ordeal of having their fingerprints scraped away with a scalpel. As Karpis recalled, "He really took the meat off." Karpis paid an extra $250 to have some work done on his face. He said it needed "patching up" after the beating the Kansas City police had given him in 1930.

Finally, when all the blood-soaked cotton swabbing had been cleaned away and the outlaws' hands and Karpis's face were a mass of bandages, Doc Moran pronounced the operations a success. The patients would soon have cause to disagree. One of Freddie's thumbs became infected and swelled into what Karpis called "a pulpy mess." Karpis was left with permanent facial scars .

For the time being, Karpis and Barker were more concerned about keeping out of the hands of the police than they were about settling accounts with Doc Moran. They went to Toledo, Ohio, to lay low for a while. Sometime later, a hoodlum associate named Harry Campbell was bitten by a dog and was fearful of rabies. Alvin and Freddie arranged for Doc Moran to travel to Toledo to give Campbell an anti-rabies shot. After treating Campbell, Moran hung around Toledo, drinking in the bars and visiting the brothels. He bragged that he was a big-time underworld doctor who had notorious bank robbers in the palm of his hand because he had worked on their faces and fingers. Word of Moran's drunken blabbering got back to Barker and Karpis.

Years later, Karpis claimed to have known nothing about Doc Moran's fate until well after the deed had been done. He said that Freddie told him that he and his brother Doc Barker (who by that time was out of prison) had taken care of Doc Moran. "Doc and I shot the son-of-a-bitch," Freddie allegedly told Karpis. "We dug a hole in Michigan and dropped him in and covered the hole with lime. I don't think anybody's ever going to come across Doc Moran again."

That, at least, was Karpis's story. However, on September 26, 1935, a badly decomposed body washed up near Crystal Beach on the Ontario shore of Lake Erie and was reported to Canadian police. They suspected that the corpse, which was missing its hands and feet, had floated over from the American side, so they contacted the FBI. Through dental records, the remains were identified as those of Dr. Joseph P. Moran. Police believed, but could never prove, that Karpis and Freddie Barker took Doc Moran for a one-way boat ride on Lake Erie. They killed him and dumped the body overboard, no doubt thinking the lake would hide it forever.

Doc Barker's parole was obtained through the efforts of Jack Glynn, a sleazy private detective hired by Alvin and Freddie. Glynn knew whom to bribe in order to spring a "lifer" like Doc. On September 10, 1932, Doc walked out of the Oklahoma state penitentiary a free man. One of the conditions of his parole was that he never again set foot in Oklahoma. Doc lost no time in joining the gang in St. Paul.

Doc Barker was about an inch shorter than Freddie, but stockier, with a neatly trimmed moustache and black hair that he combed straight back. Karpis described him as harmless-looking but "a lethal operator". Like his brother, Doc had an itchy trigger finger.

With the arrival of Doc, the Barker-Karpis outfit was now one of the most formidable of the Depression Era bandit gangs. On September 23, less than two weeks after Doc's release, they robbed the State Bank & Trust Company in Redwood Falls, Minnesota, of $35,000. They struck again on September 30, looting the Citizens National Bank of Wahpeton, North Dakota, of $7,000.

Karpis and the Barkers considered themselves professionals in a dangerous trade. They planned their heists with military precision. Every man involved in a hold-up knew his part, and timing was essential. A gang member would "case" the targeted bank while changing a large bill for smaller ones. Robbery plans were discussed in places where they couldn't possibly be overheard, such as a car parked in an otherwise deserted location. The gang "ran the roads" in the vicinity of the proposed raid until they were familiar with the streets and alleyways of the town and knew every highway, country road, and gravel track in the countryside. They marked distances from one point to another and noted the locations of landmarks like farmhouses and barns as a precaution against getting lost. They stashed cans of gasoline along escape routes. In the event of a getaway car's gas tank being punctured by police bullets, the outlaws carried corks to plug up the holes. There might even be a thermos of coffee and a bag of sandwiches at a gasoline stop.

The outlaws liked to spend their loot on luxuries like sporty cars (which they bought under false names) and fine clothes. But for their bank jobs, they used stolen cars with the original license plates removed and replaced with stolen plates. When the gang went into a small town to pull a robbery, they were dressed so as to blend in with the local people, wearing inconspicuous clothing such as farmer's overalls.

There is not a shred of evidence that Ma Barker ever participated in the planning or execution of a robbery, although she was certainly aware of what her sons and their companions were up to. Freddie and Doc hauled her around the Midwest with them as they tried to stay one jump ahead of the law. When they had a house or apartment to live in, Ma did the cooking. At other times, when the gang had a series of robberies lined up and would have to move fast, the boys would set Ma up in a hotel room in Chicago or some other large city. She would spend her time listening to hillbilly music on the radio, doing jigsaw puzzles (which were all the rage at that time), going to movies, and playing bingo. Ma's dutiful sons always made sure she had money. There was only one cause of friction between Ma and the boys: she was jealous of their girlfriends. Ma wanted to be the only important woman in Freddie's and Doc's lives and regarded all of the women with whom they had relationships as "hussies".

Sometimes a robbery went as smooth as clockwork. The gang would be in and out of the bank in minutes and be out of town before local police could respond. But the very unpredictable nature of the business made it inevitable that on some occasions, even the most carefully laid plans would go awry.

In the Wahpeton hold-up, police were alerted to the robbery-in-progress and quickly blocked escape routes out of town. The bandits grabbed two female employees and forced them to ride on the running boards of the getaway car as human shields. The police held their fire when the car pulled away from the bank, but as it headed out of town, they blasted at the rear tires with shotguns. Buckshot tore into rubber and hit the back of the car with a racket like hailstones. The two women screamed. One of them tried to jump off as the driver accelerated to fifty miles an hour, but Devol reached out a window and grabbed her around the waist.

The car was running on the rear rims by the time it swung down a side road. There, the fleeing outlaws encountered a posse that was attempting to head them off. Fearful of hitting the hostages, the posse let the getaway car pass without firing a shot. But before the bandits had gone a hundred yards, one man opened fire with a rifle. A bullet struck one of the women in the leg. She screamed in pain, but the driver didn't slow down.

The bullet- and buckshot-riddled car finally stopped in a farm field near a schoolhouse the bandits had marked on their pre-planned escape route. Karpis gave the wounded woman a shot of morphine from the gang's medical kit. He told the other woman not to blame them but "the trigger-happy bastard who fired at the car." The outlaws left the women at the schoolhouse and made good their escape in another car.

For the next two-and-a-half years, the Barker-Karpis gang was one of the most prolific criminal bands in the United States, knocking off bank after bank in daring daytime raids. They were also among the most ruthless. John Dillinger, for all his notoriety, was blamed for the murder of just one police officer, and not all crime historians agree that he was actually responsible for that homicide. The Barker brothers, Karpis, and gang members like Lawrence Devol ran up a high casualty list of slain and wounded law enforcement officers. The victims were either killed in gun battles or taken captive and executed in cold blood. Innocent civilians were also shot in the course of robberies and getaways, some of them fatally. Karpis never accepted responsibility for any of the bloodshed. In his recollections, it was always the fault of the police, other gang members who were too trigger-happy, or even the victims themselves. The idea didn't seem to have occurred to Karpis that using hostages as human shields was cowardly.

During their spree of robbery and murder, Karpis and the Barkers encountered some of the most notorious desperadoes of the era: John Dillinger, Pretty Boy Floyd, Baby

Face Nelson, and Bonnie and Clyde. Karpis liked Nelson, whom the police and society in general considered a homicidal maniac. But he scorned Bonnie and Clyde as rank amateurs. One part-time member of the Barker-Karpis gang was Verne Miller, who allegedly was a gunman in the Kansas City Massacre of June 17, 1933, in which Jelly Nash and four police officers were killed.

One of the greatest ironies of the Dirty Thirties is that more money was stolen through graft, corruption, and embezzlement at the highest political, financial, and corporate levels in any one given year than was looted from banks in hold-ups and burglaries throughout the entire Depression Era. But crooks who wore tailored three-piece suits and stole millions with the stroke of a pen didn't capture the public imagination in the way the automobile bandits did. Top law enforcement officers like FBI Director J. Edgar Hoover wouldn't even admit that criminal organizations like the Mafia existed in America. There was much more publicity to be gained from hunting down the bank robbers.

The media turned the bandits into "celebrity criminals," splashing their names across newspaper front pages and interrupting radio programs with special bulletins about their latest crimes. In movie theatres, audiences watched newsreel footage about "public enemies" before the big screen came alive with Hollywood's wildly popular gangster films featuring stars like James Cagney, Humphrey Bogart, and Edward G. Robinson. The colourful nicknames attached to some of the desperadoes were pure gold to headline writers. They could sell a lot more newspapers with stories about "Baby Face" Nelson, "Pretty Boy" Floyd, and "Machine Gun" Kelly than they could with such names as Lester Gillis, Charlie Floyd, and George Barnes.

Alvin Karpis went by several aliases, most notably "Raymond Hadley." Years after his final arrest, fellow prison inmates still called him "Ray." In his bank-robbing heyday, Karpis's criminal pals called him "Slim." But that wasn't a moniker that made eye-catching headlines. Alvin joined "Baby Face," "Pretty Boy," and "Machine Gun" in the press and in criminal lore as "Creepy" Karpis and "Old Creepy."

The origin of the name is disputed. The most commonly told story is that Karpis's scarred face gave him a sinister "creepy" appearance. However, Karpis personally told crime historian Robert Livesey, (co-author of *On The Rock*, the story of his years in Alcatraz), that a police officer coined the name. During a car chase, when Karpis was able to elude his pursuers and escape like a phantom, the policeman allegedly remarked, "That guy is creepy."

The third explanation is that the name was a media invention. *Creepy* was an eye-grabber, and it made for a striking alliteration when paired with *Karpis. Old Creepy* sold newspapers. J. Edgar Hoover liked it because it had a negative connotation. It's doubtful if the Barkers or any of Karpis's criminal associates ever called him *Old Creepy* to his face. In spite of his own self-serving version of how he got the name, Karpis probably hated being called Creepy as much as his notorious colleagues objected to being called Baby Face and Pretty Boy.

While Freddie and Doc had to deal with Ma's resentment of their girlfriends, Karpis had no such problem. There were several women in his life, but due to the nature of his "profession," the relationships were usually fleeting. In later life, Karpis admitted, "When they hooked up with me, they just naturally bought trouble." Karpis had a son by one woman (the child was raised by Alvin's parents) and married another. But wedded bliss lasted only a couple of months. Karpis left his wife, and she eventually divorced him.

Police were learning the outlaws' ways and became more skilled at tracking them down. J. Edgar Hoover declared a "war on crime" and targeted the Public Enemies. He orchestrated a publicity campaign that highlighted the bank robbers as the greatest threat to law and order in America, with his FBI "G Men" as the principal line of defence against them. In the little Midwestern towns that the automobile bandits preyed on, vigilante groups were formed to assist the small police departments. The armed shopkeepers and farmers generally proved to be ineffective at preventing robberies and capturing criminals. If anything, they provided the gunmen with more targets to shoot at.

Kidnappers

In April 1933, a St. Paul hoodlum named Jack Peifer who had strong mob connections offered the Barker-Karpis gang a big-money alternative to bank robbery: kidnapping! Snatching wealthy victims and holding them for ransom was a lucrative underworld enterprise. Former bootlegger Verne Sankey had successfully kidnapped, on separate occasions, businessmen Haskell Bohn and Charles Boettcher II and apparently made a clean getaway with the loot. (He would be arrested in 1934 and commit suicide in a jail cell.) Nonetheless, it was risky. The kidnapping and subsequent murder of aviation hero

Charles Lindbergh's baby son in 1932 had resulted in a storm of public outrage. Any kidnapping was sure to bring in the FBI. Karpis also had concerns about working with the kind of big city racketeers Peifer rubbed shoulders with. They had a history of knocking off hired gunmen whom they suspected might talk if captured.

But Peifer's proposed victim wasn't a child. The target was William Hamm Jr., president of the Hamm Brewing Company. The payoff Peifer dangled before their eyes was irresistible to Freddie and Alvin: $100,000! It would be divided amongst Peifer and his men and participating members of the Barker-Karpis gang.

Peifer's contribution to the kidnap team was a pair of former Al Capone gunmen, Shotgun George Zeigler and Byron "Monty" Bolton. They had been involved in the plot that erupted into the St. Valentine's Day Massacre in 1929. They had fallen on hard times since Big Al's demise and needed money, but Karpis respected them as professionals. Joining Freddie and Alvin in the scheme were Doc Barker and an old-time hoodlum in his sixties named Chuck Fitzgerald who had participated in a few Barker-Karpis gang bank robberies. Fitzgerald was grey-headed and had a distinguished look about him that would make him a key player in the kidnap plot.

Thirty-nine-year-old William Hamm Jr. was a millionaire bachelor. His family-owned brewery had survived Prohibition by making soft drinks and was raking in profits now that the sale of beer was once again legal. The kidnappers were counting on him having access to plenty of cash quickly and without complications.

Karpis and his confederates spent weeks planning the job. They studied the layout of the Hamm Brewery in St. Paul and Hamm's mansion, just a short walk up a hill. After watching Hamm day after day, they knew so much about him and his routine that Karpis later remarked, "I was sick of him long before the kidnapping."

The gang decided that the best opportunity to abduct Hamm was at noon when, without fail, he would walk up the hill to his house for lunch. Peifer "put the fix in" with his contacts in the St. Paul Police Department. Freddie objected to cops being involved, but Peifer explained that his paid informants would tip them off if the police planned a trap when they went to pick up the ransom money.

On June 15, as Hamm stepped out of the brewery to walk home for lunch, a grey-haired man in a business suit got out of a Hudson sedan parked across the street and approached him. The driver, Karpis, wore a chauffeur's uniform. Hamm didn't notice two men, Doc and Bolton, loitering nearby.

Fitzgerald stepped up to Hamm with his hand extended and said, "Mr. Hamm, I wonder if I might speak to you on a rather important business matter."

As he shook Hamm's hand, Fitzgerald kept talking and guided him toward the car. Before the unsuspecting victim realized what was happening, he was sitting in the car. Moments later, the two other men got in. Doc sat in the front with Karpis. Hamm was trapped in the back between Fitzgerald and Bolton. As the Hudson pulled away, Fitzgerald politely told the bewildered prisoner to get down on the floor and keep quiet.

The kidnappers drove to a location where Freddie and Zeigler were waiting with another car. They had typed ransom notes that they instructed Hamm to sign. The notes demanded $100,000 and detailed how the money was to be delivered. They carried a warning not to involve the police.

The whole operation had gone so smoothly that Hamm still didn't seem to fully understand that he had been kidnapped and could be in mortal danger. He didn't resist as Doc taped cotton balls over his eyes and then put dark glasses on him. For the next few days, Hamm had no idea where he was, and the thought must have finally occurred to him that he might not return to his mansion in St. Paul. However, the gang wanted money, not a dead millionaire.

The kidnappers drove to the Chicago suburb of Bensenville, Illinois, where they used the home of the local postmaster, Edmund Bartholmey, as a hideout. They'd figured that would be one of the least likely places anyone would suspect. Bartholmey was being paid for the use of his house and had sent his family away to visit relatives. He and Hamm didn't set eyes on each other the entire time that Hamm was in the house.

Hamm was kept in an upstairs bedroom that had the window boarded over. He wasn't allowed out except to use the bathroom. Karpis was Hamm's twenty-four-hour-a-day guard. He later said that Hamm was "an okay guy" who didn't give him any trouble and was mainly concerned about being away from the brewery at a busy time of the year.

With the window sealed, the room was hot, so Karpis provided Hamm with an electric fan. He gave him books and newspapers and brought him his food. Karpis even gave Hamm an occasional bottle of beer. That brought about a humorous moment in an otherwise tense atmosphere while everyone waited for news of the ransom.

The beer in the house wasn't from Hamm's brewery, and Karpis didn't want to offend his model prisoner by giving him a competitor's product, so he washed the labels off the bottles. Hamm drank the beer without comment. After a couple of days, Karpis became curious. "Can you tell by the taste if it's your beer?" he asked.

Hamm laughed and said, "That's a good question." After sniffing the beer, tasting it again, and holding it up to the light, the beer baron said, "I always say that Hamm's is the best, but to tell you the truth, I don't know what the hell brand this beer is."

Freddie and Zeigler handled the delivery of the ransom notes. William Dunn, vice president of sales for the brewery, collected the cash and arranged for it to be delivered, as instructed, by a brewery truck to a certain location along a specified stretch of highway. But in spite of the kidnappers' warning, Hamm's mother informed the police. Dunn didn't know that the police had his phone tapped.

A few hours before Freddie and Ziegler were to have left for the pick-up, they had a phone call from Peifer. "Don't meet the truck." Peifer's police contacts had learned that a cop with a machine gun was going to be hidden under the tarpaulin over the back of the truck.

Freddie and Ziegler didn't go for the pick-up. They contacted Dunn again and, with threats of dire consequences if they weren't obeyed, made new arrangements. This time the money was to be delivered by Dunn himself, driving a Chevrolet coupe with all of the side doors and the cover of the trunk removed. There must be no sign of police anywhere, on the road, in the fields, or in the air. The plan worked, and Freddie and Ziegler returned to the postmaster's house with a suitcase full of money. Karpis recalled later, "My God, we were happy that day."

Still, Karpis was concerned that the bills might be marked. He secretly took four twenty-dollar bills from Hamm's wallet, and replaced them with bills from the ransom money. If Hamm spent them and the newspapers reported that some of the loot had started turning up in the St. Paul area, the gang would know that they would have to be cautious with the rest of the money.

To Karpis, this was one example of how a clever criminal could outwit the police. He didn't know that a new development in fingerprint recovery using silver nitrate allowed investigators to lift prints from paper surfaces. He and Freddie had not yet had their fingers worked on by Doc Moran. The police working on the Hamm kidnapping case soon had the fingerprints of everyone who had touched the ransom notes.

On the evening of June 19, the day the ransom had been paid, Karpis, Doc, and Bolton covered Hamm's eyes with cotton and dark glasses and put him in a car. The original plan had been to drive him back to St. Paul and release him there, but Karpis thought that would be too risky. Instead, they drove all night until they were a few miles from the little town of Wyoming, Minnesota, at about eight o'clock the next morning. The kidnappers stopped the car and let Hamm, who was still blindfolded, get out. The car roared away, leaving him at the side of the road. When Hamm uncovered his eyes, he didn't have the faintest idea where he was. He walked to the nearest farmhouse to phone for help and let his family know that he was free and unharmed.

The gang still had concerns that the ransom money might be marked. Karpis flew to Reno, Nevada, where, for a fee of $5,000, he exchanged the money with criminals who specialized in laundering "hot" currency. Then he rejoined his confederates in Chicago to split up the loot.

The kidnappers now had untraceable money, but they spent a few anxious weeks worrying that at any moment the cops would close in on them. There had been a couple of other highly publicized kidnappings, and the heat was on as police searched everywhere for the perpetrators. J. Edgar Hoover had ordered his agents to put the pressure on "every known crook in the business."

The Hamm kidnappers got an unexpected break in July when police in Wisconsin apprehended a notorious criminal named Roger Touhy and three of his gang members. A search of their car turned up handcuffs, rolls of adhesive tape, and guns -- all tools of the kidnapper's trade. Hoover officially announced that the kidnappers of William Hamm Jr. were in custody. The real culprits could now relax and spend their money. Evidence would eventually prove the Touhy gang innocent of that particular crime – to Hoover's great embarrassment. But for the time being, Karpis and the Barkers could gloat over what they considered a perfect crime.

The Barker-Karpis gang had made more money from the Hamm kidnapping than most bandits could expect to grab in a dozen armed robberies. And they'd done it without white-knuckle car chases, dodging police bullets, or shooting anyone who got in their way. They could have retired from "the business". It certainly wasn't unprecedented for a crook who had pulled a big score to disappear and quietly live in comfort on his ill-gotten gains. That didn't happen with Karpis and the Barkers.

Before the summer of 1933 was over, the Barker-Karpis gang was plotting another robbery. Karpis would later claim that he was restless and craved the excitement of planning and pulling off a hold-up. But there is also a story that Frank Nitti, the mob boss who succeeded Al Capone, learned that a house in a Chicago suburb had been used as the hideout in the Hamm abduction and demanded a big cut of the ransom money because the kidnappers had trespassed on his turf. Or it could simply have been that, for men like Karpis and the Barkers, no amount of money was ever enough.

On August 30, the gang hit the Stockyards National Bank in South St. Paul. The take was $33,000, but the bandits got into a gunfight with police and bank guards. Chuck Fitzgerald was wounded in the hip and barely managed to drag himself into the getaway car. Freddie sprayed a police car with machine gun fire, hitting the two officers inside. The gang escaped through a rain of gunfire, leaving one cop dead and another disabled for life.

The robbers struck again on September 22, holding up a pair of Federal Reserve Bank messengers in Chicago. Once more the streets rang with gunfire as police and bandits shot it out. Doc was wounded in the hand, and yet another officer was killed, gunned down by Monty Bolton. When the bandits finally tore open the bank satchels they had taken from the messengers, they found only cheques absolutely worthless to them because they couldn't be cashed.

It didn't take the police long to connect the Barker-Karpis gang to the Federal Reserve fiasco, thanks to evidence found in a car they'd been forced to abandon during their escape. Meanwhile, stories were starting to hit the newspapers about the deaths or captures of notorious criminals. That July, Clyde Barrow's brother Buck had been mortally wounded in a gun battle with police. On September 26, federal agents arrested Machine Gun Kelly. Karpis began to think about running to some place far away, like Australia. That meant another big job, with a payoff on which he could retire.

Harry Sawyer approached the Barker-Karpis gang with the idea of kidnapping Edward G. Bremer, president of the

Commercial State Bank of St. Paul, and holding him for $200,000 ransom. Initially, Karpis was against it. He said he'd rather rob a bank. Bremer's father, Adolph, was a personal friend of President Franklin D. Roosevelt. Karpis was worried that with such powerful connections, the Bremer family would bring more intense police heat on the gang than they had ever known before. But Freddie scoffed, "Why are we wasting our time talking about heat? We've had nothing except heat since 1931."

Karpis gave in, having no argument with that kind of logic. The kidnap team was made up of Karpis, Freddie, Doc, Zeigler, Bill Weaver, Harry Campbell, and an old friend of Doc's named Volney Davis. As they had done with the Hamm caper, the gang planned the operation carefully. They studied the bank and Bremer's home and spent many days watching their target and noting his daily routine.

An incident that occurred about this time indicated that fear of the police had Karpis and the Barkers more than a little jumpy. Freddie and Karpis were driving through St. Paul when they saw two men in uniform in a car behind them. They immediately assumed they were being tailed by police. Freddie suddenly hit the brakes, and Karpis jumped out with a machine gun. He raked the other car with bullets, and then he and Freddie sped away. They learned the next day that the "cops" in the car Karpis had riddled were employees of Northwestern Airways, dressed in company uniforms. One of them was seriously injured, but not fatally. Recalling the incident in later years, Karpis admitted, "I'd made a bad mistake."

The kidnappers made their move on Bremer on the morning of January 17, 1934. Long after the events of that day, Karpis would say that the Bremer job was "spooked". It was not to be a repeat of the slick Hamm abduction.

Bremer had just dropped his daughter off at school and had pulled up to a stop sign when another car suddenly blocked his way. A second car stopped behind him, closing the trap. Before the startled banker knew what was happening, two strange men – Doc and Volney Davis – opened the doors of his car and forced themselves in. The plan was for them to make an obedient victim get in the back while they commandeered the car. But Bremer put up a fight, and Doc struck him on the head with a gun. The kidnappers stuffed the dazed man into the back, and then all three cars roared away.

The wound on Bremer's head was bleeding, and he was disoriented. He had trouble signing the ransom letters the gang had prepared. The kidnappers left Bremer's car in a field, blindfolded him, and drove to Bensenville where they had established a hideout in an old house. Freddie and Ziegler went to St. Paul to deliver the ransom notes while Karpis and the others waited with the prisoner.

Bremer wasn't the compliant captive Hamm had been. He complained about the conditions in which he was kept. He was afraid that someone would steal his expensive watch, a precious gift from his late mother. He pleaded with the kidnappers not to use a railway receipt he had in his pocket as proof to his family that they had him. The receipt was for a private salon for two from St. Paul to Chicago, but Bremer's wife believed he had made that trip alone. When Karpis told Bremer he was being held for $200,000, the banker surprised him by shouting, "You're crazy! My father wouldn't pay that much for me!"

According to Karpis, Bremer even tried to talk him into kidnapping another rich St. Paul businessman whose wife supposedly kept $250,000 in a safety deposit box in case her husband should be abducted. Karpis quickly took a dislike to Edward Bremer. However, he was going to have to put up with him for much longer than he had been acquainted with William Hamm.

Meanwhile, confusion swirled around the Bremer kidnapping. Police found Bremer's car and, because of the bloodstains in it, they suspected he'd been murdered. A small army of police officers and civilian volunteers dug up the field, looking for the body. Then police received a hoax letter from someone who claimed to be the kidnapper. The crank said he had killed Bremer and buried him in a snowbank in Minnesota. The letter sent police off on a wild goose chase.

President Roosevelt, in one of his famous "fireside chat" radio broadcasts, called the kidnapping "an attack on all we hold dear." Believing Bremer had been murdered, Roosevelt swore that the FBI would bring the killers to justice. J. Edgar Hoover's agents soon swarmed over St. Paul. They raided every gangster hangout and picked up every known hoodlum for questioning. The heat Karpis had worried about and Freddie had scoffed at was being applied in full force.

Freddie and Ziegler had delivered the ransom letters, but Adolph Bremer didn't respond in the way they had expected. Edward evidently knew his father well. The senior Bremer tried to negotiate the ransom down to $100,000. The kidnappers wouldn't budge on the price. Adolph refused to pay unless he had proof that his son was still alive. The gang made Bremer write letters to his father and his wife. Karpis was anxious to see the last of

Bremer, who had gone in his estimation from "a slighty miserable bastard" to "more irritating by the minute."

Adolph Bremer finally gave in. *Twenty-two days* after his son's abduction, he paid the ransom. Bremer followed instructions. He had the money, all in used five- and ten-dollar notes from a variety of issues and with no consecutive serial numbers, packed into two large suit box cartons. Then he placed a notice in the Minneapolis *Tribune* that said, "We are ready Alice." The payoff was made without any interference from the police. In one box, the kidnappers found a note from Adolph Bremer.

"To the parties holding Edward: I've done my part and kept my word 100 percent just as I said I would. This money is not marked and is the full amount asked for. And now boys, I am counting on your honor. Be sports and do the square thing by turning Edward loose at once.

(Signed) Adolph Bremer"

Before releasing Edward Bremer, Karpis made him strip off his clothes and gave him new ones. Then he burned Bremer's clothing in case it bore any clues that could be found in a crime laboratory. On the morning of February 7, Karpis, Doc, and Campbell drove a blindfolded and still complaining Bremer to a location on the highway near the town of Rochester, Minnesota, and let him out. Karpis told him to "Beat it!"

The FBI was disappointed that Bremer couldn't – or wouldn't – provide much helpful information. He said he had been blindfolded much of the time. He also claimed that the gang had threatened to kill his daughter if he talked. Nonetheless, investigators had a pretty good idea who the kidnappers were because the crime had so many similarities to the Hamm case.

Once again, Karpis was concerned that the ransom money was marked. Doc took it to Reno to make an exchange with the same gang that had laundered the Hamm ransom money. To his surprise, the Reno gangsters wouldn't touch it. The Bremer kidnapping had received so much publicity, and police activity was so intense, that the money was too hot to handle. The Barker-Karpis gang had a fortune in their hands that they could only spend at their own risk.

Karpis would later say that the Bremer money "was like a damned albatross around my neck." He and the other kidnappers could safely pass off a few bills in small purchases, but they couldn't be the big spenders they wanted to be. Doc fenced $10,000 with a Chicago racketeer, but within days the FBI, hot on the money trail, arrested the man. The gang would have to sit on the ransom money for a while yet.

Meanwhile, Karpis worked as a strong-arm man for a Cleveland gambling hall whose owners were being harassed by rivals. In addition to providing security at the hall, Karpis warned the competitors that if they gave his employers any more trouble, he would kill them, rough up their kids, and burn down their houses. The threats worked; the other hoodlums evidently wanted no part of Old Creepy.

As the months of 1934 passed, J. Edgar Hoover stepped up his war on crime. Large rewards were placed on the heads of the "public enemies". Newspapers and magazines carried pictures of men like Dillinger, Floyd, Nelson, the Barkers, and Karpis. Freddie and Karpis were in a movie theatre with Ma, watching the newsreels that always preceded the feature film, when they suddenly saw their faces on the big screen. Karpis claimed later that it was the first time Ma realized that her sons were more than ordinary crooks.

The FBI scored a major victory on July 22 when agents gunned down John Dillinger outside a Chicago movie theatre. A few days later, St. Paul police killed Dillinger gang member Homer Van Meter. The writing was on the wall for the bandit gangs. Karpis knew they had to do something with the ransom money quickly.

The gang contacted a Detroit racketeer who could launder the money in Cuba, a place much favoured by American gangsters. Karpis and the Barkers went for the deal. When they got out of Cleveland, they barely escaped a police trap that was set up when Freddie's girlfriend was arrested for public drunkenness and talked.

After that close call, Karpis and his colleagues had to keep on the move. They were hot, and safe places were getting harder to find. Karpis fled to Toledo, Chicago, and finally Miami. At Key West, he caught a boat to Havana. Cuba looked like a pretty inviting sanctuary for a fugitive with a lot of money.

Karpis took up residence in the resort town of Varadero, where he rubbed shoulders with American millionaires and other gangsters. Life there was good. But the spectre of the FBI was always lurking. Karpis's picture was in American crime magazines sold in Havana. In October, news reached the island that FBI agents had killed Pretty Boy Floyd. The following month, Baby Face Nelson was the next public enemy to meet a violent end, killed in a blazing gunfight that also took the lives of two FBI agents.

Karpis soon had trouble of his own. The FBI got word that some of the marked ransom bills had turned up in Havana. Karpis was tipped off that an agent had checked into the city's Parkview Hotel. He was asking questions and showing people pictures that included a mug shot of Karpis. It was December 1934 and time for Alvin to get out of Cuba.

Not long after slipping back into the United States, Karpis joined Freddie and Ma at Lake Weir, Florida, where they had rented a cottage. Alvin and Freddie enjoyed some leisurely days fishing and planning bank robberies. Then in mid-January 1935, Karpis went off with Harry Campbell to Little River where they spent a few days mackerel fishing. They were about to drive back to Lake Weir when they heard the stunning news that Ma and Freddie were dead.

The demise of the Barker-Karpis gang began on January 8, when Doc was arrested in Chicago. He wouldn't talk, but a letter from Ma in his possession eventually directed the FBI to Lake Weir. On the morning of January 16, a large force of federal agents surrounded the cottage.

When the police called for the occupants to surrender, they didn't know exactly who was inside the two-storey building, only that it was a Barker-Karpis gang hideout. Any of the gang's known gunmen, including Old Creepy himself, might have been in there, armed, cornered, and ready to fight. The call was answered with machine gun fire from an upstairs bedroom window. While bullets clipped the trees they used for cover, the agents replied with a fusillade of lead, pouring more than 1,500 rounds into the wooden frame structure. After about four hours, the shooting from the window stopped, but the agents waited another forty-five minutes before sending a local man who had been friendly with the Barkers into the cottage.

Ma and Freddie were both lying dead in the upstairs bedroom. Ma had been shot three times. Freddie was riddled with more than a dozen bullets. A machine gun lay on the floor between the bodies, and a pistol was near Freddie's hand.

Except for that one instance when Ma had been wanted for questioning after the murder of Arthur Dunlop, she had not been the object of any police attention. There was no warrant for her arrest. Months earlier, during the hunt for the Dillinger gang, the FBI had been embarrassed when a raid on a lodge at Little Bohemia, Wisconsin, had resulted in civilian casualties. Now federal agents had killed an old woman.

To head off criticism and bad press, Hoover reported that Ma had participated in the battle, blasting away at the agents with a machine gun. That weapon, he claimed, was found clutched in her cold, dead hands. Hoover embellished this fabrication with the story that Ma had been the leader of the gang and the brains behind its lawless exploits. He described Ma as "the most vicious, dangerous, and resourceful criminal brain of the last decade." That was the beginning of the myth of "bloody" Ma Barker.

Public Enemy # 1 and Alcatraz

The FBI now declared Alvin Karpis Public Enemy Number One. Knowing the fate that had befallen the previous bearers of that unwanted distinction – Dillinger, Floyd, and Nelson – Karpis had no time to mourn the loss of Freddie and Ma. As he admitted many years later, he was scared.

Karpis and Campbell fled to Atlantic City, New Jersey. There, on January 20, FBI agents thought they had them cornered in a hotel, but the outlaws shot their way out of the trap. Amazingly, no one was killed, and only one agent was wounded.

In their flight from New Jersey, Karpis and Campbell car-jacked an automobile in

Pennsylvania and took the doctor who owned it captive. The vehicle's medical license plates helped them bluff their way past a police roadblock. The doctor was released unharmed in Wadsworth, Ohio.

Police found the doctor's car abandoned in Monroe County, Michigan, on January 22. The location on the Lake Erie shore caused them to suspect that Karpis might be trying to escape to Canada and reach his native city of Montreal. The Ontario Provincial Police watched the border from Windsor to Amhertsburg. OPP constables searched cottages along the Canadian shore of Lake Erie in case Karpis had already sneaked across and was in hiding. They found nothing, but the newspaper articles drew Canadian readers to the unfolding drama about the Montreal-born bandit.

Doc's arrest and Freddie's death effectively ended the Barker-Karpis gang's reign of terror. Old Creepy was still on the loose, but he was the most hunted man in America. Nonetheless, even as he was being sought as Public Enemy Number One, Karpis pulled off two more sensational robberies.

On April 24, Karpis and a newly organized gang robbed a mail truck in Warren, Ohio, of $72,000. They revived memories of Wild West outlaws like Frank and Jesse James when, on November 7, they looted a train of $34,000 at Garnettsville, Ohio. Karpis might have been starting to believe that he was living a charmed life. But the fact that he was still at large had become a major thorn in the side of J. Edgar Hoover.

Hoover had been getting a lot of publicity because of the FBI's successes against the bandit gangs and had taken most of the credit himself. But his detractors pointed out that it was the agents in the field who took all the risks and sometimes died in the line of duty. Hoover had never personally made an arrest. He claimed that he'd received a death threat from Karpis that swore vengeance for the killings of Freddie and Ma. However, Hoover never produced proof of such a threat, and Karpis would deny he had ever made it. Nonetheless, Karpis presented Hoover with an opportunity to silence his critics – if his agents could locate the desperado and he could orchestrate a capture – or killing - in which he could be seen taking a leading role.

While Hoover fretted over how he could make Karpis his key to personal glory, the fugitive had become a phantom. Karpis was constantly on the move, never staying in one place long enough for police to zero in on him. He ran from hideout to hideout, in state after state – Oklahoma, Texas, Arkansas, Tennessee,

Mississippi, Florida – never certain whom he could trust, always looking over his shoulder, ever fearful that FBI agents would burst into a room in which he was sleeping or shoot him down in an ambush.

Karpis knew through newspaper reports that Hoover's forces were searching for him in almost every state in the country. There were some embarrassing blunders. FBI agents raided an apartment house in New York City after receiving a tip that Karpis was inside and mistakenly arrested an innocent man. Hordes of agents swarmed through known Karpis stomping grounds, like St. Paul, Chicago, and Cleveland, but came up empty-handed. As Karpis read the newspaper accounts, he was amused at the frustrations of the FBI. Months passed, 1935 gave way to 1936, and Old Creepy was still free. But for how long?

As weeks passed with no sign of Karpis, Hoover came under increasing pressure from the federal government. At a United States Senate hearing in April, Senator Kenneth McKellar of Tennessee tore into Hoover over the performance of the FBI. There had been blunders. There were rumours that the deaths of some of the public enemies had in fact been executions. It was a low point for the Director. But Hoover wouldn't have to wait long to vindicate himself.

On the morning of May 1, FBI agents in New Orleans located an apartment house where Karpis was holed up with a hoodlum named Fred Hunter. Hunter had been part of the train robbery gang, and it was he who inadvertently led the agents to the hideout. Hoover was informed, and he immediately flew to New Orleans. By five o'clock that afternoon, heavily armed federal agents had the building surrounded. The New Orleans Police Department was not told of the operation. That wasn't unusual. Hoover was worried that crooked cops might tip off the fugitives. But he also was jealous when it came to the FBI having to share glory with other law enforcement organizations.

Just what happened that spring afternoon in New Orleans has been a matter of dispute. According to the FBI version, Karpis and Hunter came out of the building at 5:15 and got into a Plymouth coupe. Karpis was in the driver's seat. J. Edgar Hoover suddenly reached through the open window, grabbed Karpis to prevent him from reaching for a rifle on the back seat, and ordered his men to "Put the cuffs on Karpis."

In his autobiography, Karpis told a different story. He said that he and Hunter had just gotten into the car when another car suddenly pulled in front. The Plymouth was immediately surrounded by FBI agents. One of them stuck a rifle at his head and said, "All right, Karpis, just keep your hands on that steering wheel."

The other agents had machine guns and pistols trained on the Plymouth. With everybody's attention on Karpis, Hunter quietly slid out through the passenger door and started walking away, but he was quickly stopped. The agent with the rifle told Karpis to get out of the car and keep his hands in the air. Karpis obeyed, and the agent asked him if he was carrying a gun. Karpis said no, their guns were in the trunk. Then someone shouted, "We've got him! We've got him! It's all clear, Chief." J. Edgar Hoover then stepped from around a corner to take official charge of the arrest.

Naturally, Karpis would want to discredit Hoover by saying the FBI boss didn't show himself until it was safe to do so. But at least one part of Hoover's version is an obvious fabrication. He couldn't have prevented Karpis from reaching for a rifle on the back seat because the Plymouth coupe didn't have a back seat. There were also no cuffs to put on Karpis. In all of their careful planning of the operation, none of the agents had thought to bring handcuffs. One of them had to use his necktie to bind the hands of Public Enemy Number

One. Could it have been that the agents actually thought they would have no need of handcuffs?

Karpis was taken to the FBI headquarters in New Orleans. There (according to Karpis), one of his captors told him that the police were prepared to "shoot that goddamned place apart when you surprised us by walking out the front door ... another few minutes and it would have been filled with gas and bullets ... Count yourself a lucky son of a bitch you're still alive."

Karpis was also lucky that he was never brought to trial for murder. He pleaded guilty to the Bremer kidnapping and received a sentence of life imprisonment. In August 1936, Karpis was sent to the maximum security penitentiary that had been built to hold America's most dangerous criminals: Alcatraz. It would be his residence for the next twenty-five years. As Karpis began his long stay on "the Rock", J. Edgar Hoover was being hailed as a national hero for the capture of Old Creepy. Karpis would later write, "I made Hoover's reputation as a fearless lawman. It's a reputation he doesn't deserve."

Besides such noted criminals as Al Capone and Machine Gun Kelly, Karpis's fellow inmates included Doc Barker and Bill Weaver. Doc was shot to death while trying to escape on January 13, 1939. Weaver died in the prison in

1944. Other former Barker-Karpis gang members and associates who received long prison terms in Alcatraz or elsewhere were Francis Keating, Tommy Holden, Harvey Bailey, Harry Campbell, Byron Bolton, Charles Fitzgerald, Volney Davis, and Fred Hunter.

Several of Karpis's other associates met with violent ends. Lawrence Devol was killed in a gunfight with police in 1936. Verne Miller was murdered in 1933 and George Zeigler in 1934. Jack Peifer was sentenced to thirty years in prison but committed suicide in a jail cell by swallowing cyanide poison. His ghost is said to haunt St. Paul's Landmark Center, which once housed the Ramsey County Courtroom.

In Alcatraz, Karpis worked in the prison bakery. He had a reputation among the inmates as a hard case and wouldn't let himself be pushed around by the other tough guys. When Alcatraz was closed in 1962, Karpis had spent more time there than any other convict. He was transferred to the McNeil Island Penitentiary in the state of Washington. In 1969, against the wishes of J. Edgar Hoover, Karpis was released from prison on parole and deported to Canada. He initially had some difficulty obtaining the documentation he needed to re-enter Canada because of the disfiguring surgery Doc Moran had done on his fingertips.

Karpis settled in Montreal and began writing his memoirs. He collaborated with Canadian journalist Bill Trent on his autobiography, which was published in Canada in 1971 as *Public Enemy Number One*, and in the United States as *The Alvin Karpis Story*. During a promotional tour, Karpis established a friendship with a representative of his Canadian publisher. However, the representative ended that relationship when she thought Karpis was giving her son advice she considered sociopathic.

Karpis moved to Spain in 1973. He began a collaboration with another Canadian writer, Robert Livesey, on a second autobiographical book, *On the Rock: Twenty-five Years in Alcatraz,* which tells of his life in prison. Among Karpis's many recollections was his association with a young inmate named Charles Manson.

Karpis died on August 26, 1979, at the age of seventy-one. No autopsy was done. The cause of death was initially ruled to be suicide by overdose of sleeping pills. But because Karpis had no apparent reason to take his own life and was looking forward to the publication of *On the Rock*, that ruling was changed to natural causes. Karpis's death might actually have been a case of "misadventure" due to an unintentionally fatal mixture of drugs and alcohol. He died unrepentant for the life he had led. As he wrote in the closing line of *Public Enemy Number One*, "What happened happened."

Georges Lemay: Tunnel Man

In the 1950s and '60s, stick-up men hit Montreal banks and businesses so frequently, the city had the reputation of being the armed robbery capital of Canada. There was a standing joke among Montrealers that, if you were walking along a street and saw a parked armoured car, it was a good idea to cross the road to the opposite sidewalk, just in case of a robbery. You didn't want to get caught in the crossfire between the bandits and the guards. However, there was one Montreal gangster who preferred other means of getting his hands on loot.

On the morning of Tuesday, July 4, 1961, employees of a branch of the Bank of Nova Scotia at the corner of St. Catharine Street West and St. Alexander Street returned to work after the Dominion Day long weekend. When one of them went down to the basement to the vault that housed the safety deposit boxes, he was stunned to find a gaping hole in the four-foot-thick reinforced concrete floor. In the long rows of safety deposit boxes, 377 drawers were open and empty.

The burglars had timed the job well. There was no watchman on duty from early Sunday morning until late Sunday night. Because of the holiday, they would have plenty of time to pull the job and make their getaway. They even seemed to be aware that the July 1 weekend had been scheduled for a re-structuring of the chain of command in the investigative branch of the Montreal Police Department. That meant detectives might be slow off the mark in getting on the robbers' trail. Due to the secrecy concerning the contents of safety deposit boxes and the tendency of some of the robbery victims to exaggerate their losses for insurance claim purposes, reports on the total value of the plunder ranged from $633,000 to four million dollars in cash, jewelry, and negotiable bonds.

Montreal police detective Leo Plouffe told reporters the robbery was an expert job. That was an understatement. The heist had been so expertly planned and executed that, after months of investigation, the police didn't have a substantial clue as to who was responsible. Only a lucky break gave them a lead.

In January 1962, forty-year-old Jaques Lajoie, a Montreal hoodlum with a long criminal record, was arrested on a charge unrelated to the bank robbery. Expecting that his previous troubles would net him a long prison term, Lajoie decided to turn informer. He said he had broken into the Bank of Nova Scotia with three other men who were well known to the Montreal police: Roland Primeau and brothers Andre and Yvon Lemieux. According to Lajoie, they crawled through a storm drain viaduct that ran under the bank building. Then, with only flashlights to see by, they cut their way up through the concrete with drills, chisels, and crowbars.

While the four men laboured and sweated underground, the gang leader who had planned the heist was in a building across the street. Seated by a window, he watched through binoculars for any sign of the police. He directed the operation by means of a walkie-talkie.

Early in the morning of Sunday, July 2, the tunnelers broke through the floor into the vault. They informed the leader, who quickly joined them via the subterranean passage. He was a skilled safecracker who easily picked open the locks of the safety deposit boxes. The five thieves hauled their swag back through the tunnel, then drove away in cars that had been parked in a nearby alley.

Lejoie told police that he'd been promised $10,000 for his part in the robbery but had been paid only $3,500. He was therefore willing, in return for leniency, to give them the name of the mastermind. It was yet another name with which the Montreal police were familiar: Georges Lemay.

Born in Shawinigan, Quebec, on January 25, 1925, Lemay was a son of well-to-do parents. He went to good schools and, at one time, even considered going into the priesthood. However, as a youth in a parochial college, Lemay developed a taste for the pleasures of life that he never would have been able to satisfy if he'd donned a cassock. He loved the playboy lifestyle. Though he drank and gambled only in moderation, Lemay enjoyed visiting Montreal's popular nightspots and hanging out with the high rollers. He was a woman chaser who would often try to pick up other men's dates. A fun-loving young man who knew how to turn on the charm, Lemay won friends easily. A columnist who covered the night club scene for a Montreal publication later said of Lemay, "Even if this guy had been the biggest bum going, you couldn't help but like him."

When he had finished school, Lemay went to work as a real estate agent in his mother's realty company. But the money he earned wasn't enough to pay for his expensive tastes. He liked fine clothes, sports cars, motorized sail boats, and small planes. Lemay acquired a pilot's license and once broke his nose when he crashed his plane into a lake. He had a cottage in the Laurentians and took trips to Las Vegas, Havana, and Miami. In order to support all this excess and maintain his image as a big spender, Lemay turned to burglary.

Lemay's first steps into a life of crime brought about a few minor run-ins with the police. But he had been careful – and lucky – and investigators couldn't pin anything on him. In Toronto in 1943, he was charged with receiving stolen goods but escaped from jail. Real trouble didn't come his way until 1952.

Lemay had been involved with many women, but the relationships were always short-lived. Charming though he could be, Lemay was short and stocky and not the image of the dashing Hollywood movie star he fancied himself to be. He also had a hair-trigger temper and could behave violently when angered. Emotionally, Lemay had never outgrown adolescence and wasn't inclined to pursue any long-term personal commitment. Then he met Huguette Daoust.

Strikingly attractive, twenty-one-year-old Huguette came from a prominent Montreal family. Her brother Raymond was a noted criminal attorney. Before she became acquainted with Lemay, Huguette had been a semi-finalist in the Miss Cinema beauty contest sponsored by Montreal's *Le Petit Journal*. She was also a drama student who'd had some small parts in stage and radio productions.

Georges and Huguette fell in love – or so it seemed. They were married on May 19, 1951, against the wishes of the bride's mother and brother. The newlyweds had their honeymoon in Miami.

Back in Montreal, wedded bliss quickly gave way to marital strife. Georges and Huguette frequently quarreled, quite likely because Lemay wasn't suited to the domestic life of a stay-at-home husband. Huguette no doubt saw for the first time how frightening Georges could be when he lost his temper. By Christmas, the seven-month-old marriage seemed to be headed for the rocks. Georges decided that what he and Huguette needed to re-ignite the flame was a second honeymoon. What better time for it than the Christmas-New Year season? Huguette agreed, and the couple got in their car and headed for Miami.

On the night of January 2, 1952, Lemay reported to police in Key West that his wife was missing. He said they had been fishing from a bridge of the Overseas Highway, and Huguette was wearing only shorts and a halter top. At about 10:30 pm, Lemay said, she went to get some warmer clothing from their car, which was parked 150 yards away at the side of the highway. She didn't come back.

Officers from the Florida State Police and the Key West Sheriff's Department launched a search by land, sea, and air but found no sign of the missing woman. A report that a woman answering Huguette's description had been seen on the Tamiami Trail in the Everglades turned out to be a false lead. While the search was in progress, Lemay was hysterical. Deputy Sheriff James Barker reported that at one point, Lemay "went berserk" and had to be restrained. Barker dismissed the possibility that Huguette had fallen off the bridge. He suspected she had been kidnapped. Within twenty-four hours, Canadian newspapers carried headline stories about the "Montreal Beauty" who was feared to have been kidnapped in Florida.

Raymond Daoust arrived in Miami on January 6 and went straight to the scene of his sister's disappearance. The Montreal Police Department and the Surete du Quebec (Quebec Provincial Police) had requested that the Florida authorities give Daoust every possible assistance in finding Hughuette. Daoust believed kidnapping was the only possible explanation for her disappearance. He made a public plea. "I appeal to the kidnappers to release her. She wouldn't harm anybody. I'm offering $500 reward for any clue leading to her discovery."

Lemay's car was impounded and searched, and he was questioned at Key West for two hours by Florida State Attorney J. Lancelot Lester. Satisfied that Lemay was telling the truth about Huguette's strange disappearance, Lester released him. Lemay repeated his story to waiting reporters, saying, "I was so upset, I didn't know what to do."

Daoust arrived to take Lemay to get his car out of the police pound. The two Montrealers conversed in French in the presence of the reporters. The Americans couldn't understand what was said but noted that Lemay seemed nervous and broke into tears.

That night, the manager of a Miami gas station called the police to report a man who was causing a disturbance. Two patrolmen responded and confronted Georges Lemay. The officers said he was drunk. Lemay attacked one of the cops and had to be forcefully subdued.

Lemay was taken to a hospital to have minor injuries treated, and then to a sanitarium. In the morning, Deputy Sheriff Barker arrived with another officer to take Lemay back to Key West, where the search for Huguette was still ongoing. Lemay suddenly "fought wildly" and had to be handcuffed. In spite of such erratic behaviour, he was soon released. J. Lancelot Lester said the state of Florida had no reason to hold him.

Huguette's disappearance stymied the Florida police. If she'd been kidnapped, nobody ever made a ransom demand. On January 11, Deputy Sheriff Barker told the press that his department was certain Huguette had been a victim of violence. "We are assembling additional evidence that lends credence to my original theory of an unlawful act having been committed," he said. "But I can't say a word about it."

Whatever that evidence was, nothing ever came of it. If the Florida police suspected Lemay of foul play, without a body they had no case for murder. Lemay, the broken-hearted husband, was allowed to return to Canada – alone! But before he left, United States Immigration authorities served him with a summons to appear at a hearing to determine whether he would be permitted to enter the country again. Lemay failed to appear at the hearing, so he was officially barred from entering the United States.

Eerily, almost exactly twelve years later, on January 4, 1964, remains identified as those of Huguette Lemay would be found in the waters of the Florida Keys. By that time,

Georges Lemay was the subject of an entirely different investigation, and there was still no proof she had been murdered. Any defence lawyer would have said the unfortunate woman could have fallen off the bridge after all. The circumstances of Huguette's disappearance and death remain a mystery.

Huguett LeMay ... Disappeared

Huguette Lemay

It's noteworthy that, in 1954, an ex-girlfriend of Lemay had him charged with intimidation. She told the Montreal police that he had repeatedly threatened her after she'd broken up with him. Lemay was arrested, but then the woman suddenly had a change of heart and wouldn't testify against him. The charge was dropped and Lemay was released.

After Huguette's disappearance, Lemay returned to the fast, free life of a playboy. Although his name only occasionally appeared in police reports, he was becoming a familiar figure in the Montreal underworld. He was associated with the notorious West End Gang, which was involved in robbery and racketeering. In 1955, Lemay was tried for disturbing the peace, resisting arrest, and assaulting a police officer. He was fined $25 and ordered to post a $200 peace bond. Lemay was known to be a close friend of Lucien Rivard, a burglar, gun runner, and drug smuggler. Rivard would one day make international headlines after a sensational prison break.

Lemay was still stealing to support his luxurious lifestyle and was learning the craft of picking locks and cracking safes. Most important for a man now dedicated to a criminal career, Lemay was learning how to plan and execute robberies like a professional. In January 1957, Lemay pulled his first tunneling job.

The target was the branch of the Royal Bank of Canada in the Van Horne Shopping Centre in Montreal's Outrement district. Thieves dug their way into the vault and looted safety deposit boxes of a reported two million dollars in cash, jewelry, and bonds. They escaped with the swag and were allegedly instructed by the leader to lie low until he said it was safe to fence the jewels and the bonds.

The Montreal police suspected Lemay of being the brains behind the heist but couldn't find the evidence to prove it. A hoodlum named Larry Petrov gave the cops the break they were waiting for when he ignored orders and foolishly tried to cash some of the stolen bonds. Detectives were quickly on the scent. But somebody got to Petrov before he could be picked up and questioned. On July 10, his father reported him missing.

Lemay was arrested in a raid on his cottage at Mont Rolland on July 11. Police held him for a week but couldn't produce the evidence needed to lay a charge. He was released after paying a small fine for possession of two unregistered handguns. A few days later, campers in the St. Donat region ninety miles north of Montreal discovered a human leg at the edge of a lake. It was identified as Petrov's. No one was ever charged with his murder. Lemay continued to live the high life. He considered himself too clever by far for the police – until Jacques Lajoie fingered him for the Bank of Nova Scotia robbery.

Lajoie's information led to the arrests of Roland Primeau and the Lemieux brothers, but Georges Lemay was nowhere to be found. Because of his absence, the Bank of Nova Scotia robbery case was held up in the courts for more than five years. When it finally went to trial in 1967, Primeau was sentenced to thirteen years in prison. Andre Lemieux got seven years and Yvon six years. In return for selling out his partners, Lejoie received a token sentence of one day in jail. Meanwhile, Georges Lemay had become the most wanted criminal in Canada.

After Lajoie had given them Lemay's name, police once again raided the cottage in the Laurentians, striking at dawn on January 5, 1962. Lemay wasn't there, but officers found $2,000 in American currency hidden behind a secret panel in a bedroom closet. A nationwide warrant was issued for Lemay's arrest, but investigators suspected that he had already slipped out of Canada. Knowing of Lemay's fondness for a warm climate, the Royal Canadian Mounted police wired information, including Lemay's photograph, to police departments in Florida, the Bahamas, and several South American countries. Within days, they had a response from Miami.

Weeks earlier, a man answering Lemay's description had been seen on a yacht called the *Annu* that was moored at a dock in front of the Ocean Ranch Hotel. Police following up on the tip found the boat locked up. The hotel manager told them it had been sitting there, unoccupied, since November. The *Annu* was registered to a Montreal owner. Police concluded that Lemay had borrowed the boat and sailed it to Miami. He had been living on the yacht but had abandoned it when he thought it might lead the police to him.

The discovery of the yacht sent Canadian police detectives to Miami. They assisted local police in identifying six ex-Montrealers living in Miami who were believed to have criminal connections. One of the suspects picked up in the search for Lemay was twenty-five-year-old Lise Lemieux, the sister of Andre and Yvon. She gave her occupation as "singer". Lise had been charged as an accomplice in the Bank of Nova Scotia robbery but was released after pleading guilty and serving a short term in jail.

The round-up of suspected Canadian crooks in Florida made the newspapers in Canada, but it didn't get Canadian authorities any closer to Georges Lemay. The suspects wouldn't talk, even when a $2,000 reward was dangled in front of them.

Lemay's trail was cold. For two years, police could find no clue as to his whereabouts. In August 1964, he was placed on the RCMP's "most wanted" list. Rewards for information leading to his arrest totalled $10,000. The Mounties advised the public that they considered Lemay to be armed and dangerous.

On March 2, 1965, Lemay's pal Lucien Rivard escaped from Montreal's Bordeaux jail where he was being held pending extradition to the United States to face drug smuggling charges. Rivard's jail break was a major embarrassment to the Canadian government, which was strongly criticized by Washington for failing to hold such a notorious criminal. Every law enforcement agency in Canada, from the RCMP to small-town police departments, was on the lookout for Rivard. There were rumours that he had fled the country, and he was reported to be in places as far away as Spain.

In their desperation to find Rivard, Canadian police decided to try new technology, then known as "satellite police power." Through a pioneering satellite program called Early Bird, the United States, Canada, and the United Kingdom could broadcast images of criminals wanted by the FBI, the RCMP, and

Scotland Yard. The images were seen by television viewers all over North America and in the UK. Lucien Rivard's picture was supposed to appear on American television screens. But for some reason it was replaced with Georges Lemay's.

Lemay was about to have the distinction of being the first criminal to be caught through the use of Early Bird. A boat repairman at a marina in Fort Lauderdale, Florida, recognized the face on his TV screen as that of a man he knew as Rene Roy. For the previous six months, Roy had been living on a yacht anchored at the marina. He always had a fat wad of hundred-dollar bills that he liked to flash for all to see. The repairman informed the Fort Lauderdale police. On May 5, 1965, officers staked out the yacht, took Lemay by surprise, and arrested him without a struggle. As Lemay was taken off the boat in handcuffs, an unidentified man among the bystanders said to him, "Now George, you take care of yourself. You know what I mean?"

Later, witnesses said that Lemay and that man had frequently been seen together at various places around Fort Lauderdale. His description was very much like that of Rivard. Whoever the man was, he disappeared from Fort Lauderdale after Lemay's arrest. Rivard would remain at large until July 16, when police arrested him at a cottage about twenty miles from Montreal. He would deny ever having been in Florida. Ironically, Rivard's lawyer was Raymond Daoust.

Before being taken away to the Dade County jail in Miami, Lemay paid his marina bill. He told the dock master, "I'm paying you with my own money. The money these people (the police) are interested in is somewhere else."

While he was being questioned in jail, Lemay said, "I very seldom make mistakes. How did you do it?"

When detectives explained what had led them to him, Lemay responded, "Well, isn't that something! It took a satellite to catch me."

Investigators learned that Lemay had been in the United States almost the whole four years since the Bank of Nova Scotia robbery. The previous Easter, he had gone home to Montreal for a visit. Then he had re-entered the United States at Rouses Point, New York, using a false Canadian passport.

Lemay wasn't alone on the yacht when the police moved in. With him was his girlfriend, Lise Lemieux. She, too, was arrested, and charged with being in the United States illegally. She was released on $1,000 bail, but was told not to leave Miami because she would be obliged to testify at Lemay's extradition hearing.

Reporters found Lise in a Miami hotel that was popular with French *Canadien* tourists. She agreed to be interviewed in the hotel's bar in the company of two men she said were her bodyguards. She told the reporters they didn't have to worry about those men, "as long as I'm smiling."

Lise said that Lucien Rivard had never been on their yacht, and she'd never even heard Lemay talk about him. She said that Lemay was innocent of bank robbery, that he'd made his money in the real estate business. Lise also claimed that she and Lemay had been married in Mexico.

Under American law, no husband or wife could be forced to testify against a spouse. Lise and Georges couldn't prove that they had been legally married in Mexico, so Lise applied for a Florida marriage license. Concerned that the couple might contrive a jailhouse wedding, authorities denied Lise visiting privileges and moved Lemay to an interior cell so they couldn't communicate through a window facing the street. Meanwhile, Lemay's Miami lawyer, Henry St. Jean, told United States Immigration Investigator Milton Milich that his client would fight extradition to Canada but was willing to voluntarily leave the United States under a law that allowed him to choose his destination. Lemay would go to Haiti or Mexico if either country would grant him a visa.

It certainly wasn't unheard of for cash-strapped governments of poor countries to provide sanctuary to criminals who could afford to pay for it. The Canadian government insisted that the Americans send Lemay home and not let him escape to Haiti or Mexico just so they could avoid the time and expense of extradition proceedings. Milich had no intention of letting Lemay go. His immediate response to St. Jean's request was to lay additional charges against Lemay for illegal entry and residency. Lemay would have to face an extradition hearing but, through his lawyer, he and Lise hatched a scheme that took immigration officials and police officers by surprise.

On June 1, officers escorted Lemay to the U.S. Immigration office in Miami where the hearing was to be conducted. As they waited in a small ante-room, Lise suddenly appeared with St. Jean and a Justice of the Peace. Before the officers realized what was happening, Lise and Georges exchanged matrimonial vows in French. They kissed, and the JP pronounced them man and wife. No rings were exchanged, but the marriage was legal. Now Lise could not be called upon to testify.

As clever as the on-the-spot wedding trick was, in the end it didn't help Lemay's case. Even without Lise's testimony, Milich still had enough evidence to gain a court order for Lemay to be extradited to Canada. St. Jean appealed the court's decision, and Lemay was taken back to jail to await the next hearing. Now that Lise was no longer eligible to testify, Milich re-opened the case against her as an illegal alien and began the process to have her deported. Meanwhile, Lise was still free on bail but forbidden to leave Miami. Early in August, while Lemay was still awaiting his appeal hearing, Lise checked out of her hotel and disappeared.

The odds were heavily stacked against Lemay having any success with an appeal. He had been illegally residing in a country from which he had already been barred. He was wanted by his native country as the prime suspect in a major crime. And the United States and Canada had a solid extradition agreement. Milton Milich wanted nothing more than to hand Lemay over to RCMP officers and see the last of him. Nonetheless, St. Jean kept having the hearing postponed through one legal pretext or another. Meanwhile, Lemay was working on a plan to sidestep the odds.

The Dade County jail was a modern detention facility, said to be escape-proof.

Lemay was kept in a maximum security cell on the fifth floor. For any prisoner to bypass all of the guards and get out of the building seemed impossible. But Lemay found a way.

On the night of September 21, Lemay somehow got out of his cell. Unseen by any of the jail's staff, he went to a room on the tenth floor where he picked up a 100-foot coil of strong electrical cable. Then he went down to the seventh floor. He tied one end of the cable to a plumbing fixture, broke a window, and unrolled the rest of it down the side of the building. Lemay then shimmied down the cable to the ground ninety feet below. He was seen getting into a white 1965 sedan occupied by three other persons, one of whom was believed to be a woman. The car sped away and was lost in city traffic.

As soon as Lemay was reported missing from his cell, the Miami police launched a search. Patrol cars prowled the streets and alleyways in neighbourhoods near the jail on the chance that he hadn't gone far. Detectives went to Miami Beach hangouts known to be popular with Lemay and his friends, hoping to pick up a lead on where he might be headed. Nobody the cops spoke to knew a thing, or so they claimed. Because Lemay was an experienced yachtsman who knew how to handle a boat, police watched the harbour in case he tried to escape by sea. But in spite of the massive search, Lemay made a clean getaway.

If Canadian authorities had been embarrassed over Lucien Rivard's escape from custody while awaiting extradition to the United States, now it was the Americans' turn to be red-faced. How could they have let a criminal who was so badly wanted by Canadian police slip through their fingers?

Dade County Sheriff T.A. Buchanan believed that Lemay had inside help. A search of his cell turned up hacksaw blades, a knife, gloves, and a coil of nylon rope hidden in his mattress. It wasn't reported whether or not Lemay had used the blades to cut his way out of the cell, but the items had clearly been smuggled to him, and the escape plan had obviously been in the works long before the break-out.

Most perplexing was the question of how Lemay had been able to get up to the tenth floor where he evidently knew a coil of electric cable lay waiting, and then take it down to the seventh floor, as freely as if he had the run of the jail. As was to be expected, prisoners in the other cells said that they hadn't seen a thing. But where had the guards and other jail staff been?

An anonymous Miami police lieutenant told reporters that the mystery of how Lemay got from his cell to the window through which he made his escape was "the $64,000 question." That was an inference to a popular television game show. As it turned out, the cost of Lemay's escape was $35,000 in bribe money.

The investigation into the escape led to the arrests of two jail guards and a bail bondsman who was an ex-policeman. The three men had become very friendly with Lemay. The bondsman had been seen with Lise before she dropped out of sight. Sheriff Buchanan told the press that his department had uncovered enough evidence to charge the men with accepting bribes to assist Lemay. Two other guards were fired for negligence. The investigating committee learned there had been utter confusion in the jail when the escape alarm sounded because guards didn't know what to do. The guard in charge of a hot-line telephone that had been installed for just such an emergency didn't know how to operate it.

While security measures in the Dade County jail underwent a complete overhaul, Florida police searched the length and breadth of the state for Georges and Lise Lemay but found nothing. An airline stewardess reported that she had seen a couple that looked like the fugitives on a flight that left Miami for Nassau just fourteen hours after the jailbreak. U.S. Immigration officers flew to Nassau, where local police helped them locate the suspect couple. They were the wrong people. Dade County police officials said Nassau wouldn't be a likely destination for Lemay because the Bahamas, a British colony, would be able to send him back to Canada much more quickly than U.S. Immigration officials could.

When days had passed with no sign of Lemay or Lise, Florida police were sure they were no longer in the state, and probably not even in the country. If they hadn't escaped by car or plane, they could have slipped away by boat from any one of the hundreds of coves and inlets along the Florida coast. "George Lemay has more than likely executed his own deportation order," an Immigration officer told the press.

The Americans thought Haiti the most likely place for Lemay to seek sanctuary. He had already expressed a desire to go there. It was a French-speaking country, ruled by a corrupt administration that would accept bribe money in return for asylum. Moreover, there were poor relations between Washington and Haitian dictator Francois "Papa Doc" Duvalier, who would delight in thumbing his nose at the

United States by taking in a wealthy escapee from an American jail.

For almost a year after the escape, nothing was heard of Lemay. For all the Canadian public knew, he was living like a king on his stolen money, on a Caribbean island where he was the paying guest of a notorious dictator. Some people even looked upon Lemay as an outlaw folk hero, a colourful bandit who had knocked over a rich bank and then made fools of the police in Canada and the United States. What hard-working wage-slave wouldn't like to do what Lemay had done and retire to a life of ease on a tropical island? But Lemay wasn't on a tropical island. He hadn't even left the United States. His love of the fast life would be his undoing.

Lemay's nemesis was a persistent former Montreal policeman. Inspector Joseph Bedard had been the detective in charge of the Bank of Nova Scotia investigation. Failure to apprehend Lemay had been a particular disappointment in his professional career. Bedard eventually left the police department for a position as chief of security for the Royal Bank of Canada. But he didn't give up on Lemay.

Bedard knew that Lemay was drawn to the world of night clubs, casinos, and all the other venues where big spenders spent money like it was water. He also knew that Lemay was especially fond of Las Vegas. The glittering gambling mecca of America, put on the map by mobster Benjamin "Bugsy" Siegel, was a place where gangsters rubbed shoulders with movie stars. When a man like Lemay had plenty of money, a city like Las Vegas was practically his natural habitat.

Bedard had a friend – whose name he kept confidential – who often went to Las Vegas on holidays. Bedard gave him a picture of Lemay and asked him to keep an eye out for him whenever he was there. Bedard warned his friend that if he saw someone he thought was Lemay not to approach him, because during Lemay's stay in the Dade County jail, he had allegedly said that he would shoot it out before allowing himself to be arrested again. Bedard told his friend to first contact the FBI and then call him in Montreal. On one of the friend's trips to Las Vegas, he "hit the jackpot", as Bedard later put it.

On August 19, 1966, Bedard's unofficial undercover agent spotted Georges Lemay in the Golden Nugget Casino. He recognized him even though Lemay had shaved his head bald. The man went straight to the nearest phone and called the FBI.

Agents, detectives, and police officers swarmed across the city, covering all of the casinos in case Lemay was "doing the town." But the group of agents dispatched to the Golden Nugget found him still there. Lemay was coming out of a men's washroom when they collared him.

Lemay was unarmed, so there was no shoot-out. He told the agents that they had the wrong man, that his name was Robert G. Palmer. But when he realized the game was up, he admitted who he was. Lemay asked one of the agents, "Who's a good lawyer?"

An FBI agent told the press, "He didn't offer any resistance, and although he wasn't very happy, he almost seemed to have been expecting it."

Lemay gave the officers the address of a house he'd been renting in Las Vegas. Police officers went there and arrested Lise. They also found $10,000 in American and Canadian currency. When the news hit Canadian newspapers, knocking stories about the Beatles' visit to Toronto off the front pages, Canadian readers learned that the "most wanted" couple had a four-year-old daughter.

While the child was placed in the custody of juvenile authorities, the parents were locked up in the Las Vegas jail on Florida fugitive warrants. Both still faced immigration charges, and Lemay was wanted there for escaping custody and suspicion of bribery. Lise had an additional charge of skipping bail in Miami. A Las Vegas judge now set their bail at $100,000 each. Their lawyer, Harry Claiborne, protested that the high amount set for Lise was "penalizing" and had it reduced to $10,000. However, a federal officer said that if Lise posted bail, he would immediately arrest her on an immigration warrant that carried no possibility of bail.

Lemay was offered an opportunity to waive extradition from Nevada to Florida, but he refused it. He would rather be taken back to Miami and deal with the authorities there than be sent directly to Montreal to face the music for the Bank of Nova Scotia robbery. What happened next would depend on whether Florida authorities insisted on prosecuting Lemay, or would be willing to step aside and let Nevada deport him to Canada.

After weeks of legal wrangling, the state of Florida finally agreed to let the Canadians have Lemay on the condition that if he was acquitted, he would immediately be extradited to Florida to face outstanding charges there. The Lemay family was soon back in Canada. On October 7, Lemay appeared in a Montreal courtroom where he entered no plea to the bank robbery charges. It was the beginning of a legal battle that would drag on for a year.

Meanwhile, police officials tried to debunk the myth of the smiling, dapper Georges Lemay as a bandit hero. They said there was nothing impressive about Lemay's escapades in the United States because, as they put it, "The jet age favours the fugitive."

Montreal Assistant Police Director Roland Perron told the press, "Any dope can get on a plane and flee to another country today. We've had dumbbells able to avoid capture longer than Lemay. People who manage to avoid the police for long periods get too much credit for being clever or colourful. Most of the time they're just lucky or they happen to run into a couple of crooked officials."

Lemay's preliminary hearing opened on November 21, 1966. Jaques Lajoie, the main witness for the crown, entered the courtroom with a bodyguard of four police detectives. He gave Judge Emile Trottier a sealed envelope containing information about his places of residence and employment. Lemay's defense lawyers protested this unusual procedure, but the judge and Crown Prosecutor Jean Bruneau said it was necessary "for obvious reasons."

Lajoie testified in detail how Lemay had masterminded the Bank of Nova Scotia robbery, from the planning stages through to the heist and the getaway. Lemay had purchased the equipment and explosives, Lajoie said, even going to New York City to buy the walkie-talkies. Posing as the manager of an advertising firm, Lemay had rented an office in the building across the street from the bank. That was the gang's lookout post and command centre. Lemay had obtained a key to a side door leading to the furnace room of the building in which the bank was housed. That gave the robbers access to a trap door, beneath which they began tunnelling.

Lajoie said that most of the work was done over the two weekends prior to the Dominion Day holiday, with Lemay directing every aspect of the operation. When the tunnel was almost completed, Lemay had put the gang through a dress rehearsal. He wanted to be sure that everyone knew exactly what to do.

During the final stage of the break-in, when they were blasting through the concrete floor, Lemay gave instructions from the office, through his walkie-talkie. Across the street, in the furnace room, Lajoie had the other walkie-talkie. He passed on the orders to the men in the tunnel. Each time they were about to set off a charge of dynamite, Lemay went out to the street to see if the blast could be heard. There was no sound that would alert any passers-by.

Lajoie said that after the robbery, the gang took the loot to Lemay's cottage in the

Laurentians. There, he was given a bag of money that was supposed to contain his promised share. He said he didn't count it immediately because he trusted Lemay. Only later did Lajoie realize that he'd been double-crossed. Police had gathered up the equipment the robbers left behind, and Lajoie identified the items as tools Lemay had purchased for the crime.

Lajoie had a long criminal record as a thief and a counterfeiter, so the credibility of his testimony was severely challenged in cross-examination by Guy Guerin, the senior attorney in Lemay's defense team. At several points, Lajoie either refused to answer questions or responded with angry outbursts when Guerin suggested that his memory was faulty. When he was warned by Judge Trottier that he was obliged to answer questions, Lajoie apologized for his behaviour, but added, "On the question of the bank burglary, my memory is completely faithful."

In the months that followed, the Lemay trial became a mire of postponements and deferments as the prosecution and defence tried to outmaneuver each other and raised objections over a litany of legal technicalities. Guerin learned that a $2,000 reward had been paid to an unnamed person who had assisted the police. He claimed that the defence had a right to know who that person was, but the police would not reveal the individual's identity.

Lise, who had no outstanding Canadian charges against her and so was not under arrest, sent a telegram to Provincial Justice Minister Jean Jacques Bertrand, complaining that her husband wasn't getting a fair hearing. That led to a heated exchange in the National Assembly in Quebec City when Bertrand admitted he had visited Lemay in jail. Opposition leader Jean Lesage suggested it was highly improper for a justice minister to be having friendly chats with an accused criminal whose case was still before the court. Bertrand replied that his visit had been on humanitarian grounds and he had been accompanied by Health and Welfare Minister Jean-Paul Cloutier. He angrily told the Assembly, "There will be no police state in the province of Quebec under the present minister."

Lemay exercised his right to a trial by judge rather than jury. The courtroom squabbling between the opposing counsels continued. At one point the presiding judge, Jacques Trahan, became so exasperated with the endless objections from both sides that he asked the embattled attorneys, "Do you gentlemen want to proceed with the case today, or play house?"

The Lemay trial finally ended on October 17, 1968. Dozens of witnesses had been questioned. Exhibits that included digging tools, walkie-talkies, coveralls, and dynamite blasting caps (which had caused the courtroom to be cleared for several hours) had been paraded as evidence. The trial venue had even been moved to the scene of the crime so that everyone involved could see the tunnel. Lemay had graciously helped Judge Trahan remove the trap door in the furnace room. With so much testimony to review, Trahan said he would hand down a judgement on December 6. As had practically become the norm with the Lemay case, the date was postponed, this time until January 17, 1969.

Before a packed courtroom, Judge Trahan pronounced Lemay guilty of conspiracy to commit bank burglary and the act of committing bank burglary. His judgement was meticulously outlined in a 274-page document which he took ninety minutes to read. Trahan then sentenced Lemay to eight years in prison.

It was not an especially harsh sentence, considering that Roland Primeau, who was not the leader of the gang, had received thirteen years. Nonetheless, Lemay's counsel submitted an appeal based on forty separate grounds, including what they claimed was bias on the part of the presiding judge. The appeal failed, and Lemay was packed off to prison.

The $10,000 that Lemay and Lise had in their possession when they were arrested in Las Vegas was the only part of the Bank of Nova Scotia loot that was ever recovered. What had become of all the cash, bonds, and jewelry taken from the safety deposit boxes? During the trial, a witness who had known Lemay in Miami, when he was living aboard the *Annu*, said that about the time Lemay had disappeared from the area, he had received an unusual phone call. He was told to go to the yacht and look in a certain compartment where he would find some jewelry. He was to take the jewelry and throw it into the sea. The witness claimed that he did exactly as he was instructed.

From the time of the robbery until his final arrest in Las Vegas, Lemay certainly squandered a lot of money living the high life. But was the $10,000 all that was left of his share of the swag? Did he have a stash somewhere that the police never found, or was he planning to pull another big job when the funds ran out?

In January of 1970, Lise announced that she was filing for divorce, claiming that Lemay no longer wished to be married to her. Lemay was paroled in 1975. A short time later,

Montreal police picked him up on suspicion of burglary. He was questioned and then released.

On January 26, 1979, Lemay and a man named Pierre Quintal were arrested in Riviere-des-Prairies on charges of manufacturing LSD. Quintal was shot dead on May 9 outside his lawyer's office. For years, police had no solid leads in the case. Then on October 17, 1983, they arrested Lemay and three other men for conspiracy to commit murder. However, the Crown couldn't satisfy a jury as to their guilt, and all four were acquitted.

Georges Lemay lived out his last years in obscurity. He died in his Montreal home on September 28, 2008, at the age of 82. The bulk of the loot from the Bank of Nova Scotia burglary has never been recovered.

Acknowledgments

Thank you to my editor, proof-readers, and cover artist for your support:

- - Edward

Aeternum Designs (book cover), Bettye McKee (editor), Dr. Peter Vronsky and RJ Parker Publishing, VP Publications, Lorrie Suzanne Phillippe, Marlene Fabregas, Darlene Horn, Ron Steed, Katherine McCarthy, Robyn MacEachern, Lee Knieper Husemann, Kathi Garcia, Vicky Matson-Carruth, and Linda H. Bergeron

Books in the Crimes Canada Collection

An exciting 24-volume series collection, edited by crime historian Dr. Peter Vronsky and true crime author and publisher RJ Parker.

VOLUMES:

(URL LINK ON NEXT PAGE)

- Robert Pickton: The Pig Farmer Killer by C.L. Swinney

- Marc Lepine: The Montreal Massacre

by RJ Parker

- Paul Bernardo and Karla Homolka
  by Peter Vronsky

- Shirley Turner: Doctor, Stalker,
  Murderer
  by Kelly Banaski

- Canadian Psycho: Luka Magnotta
  by Cara Lee Carter

- The Country Boy Killer: Cody
  Legebokoff
  by JT Hunter

- The Killer Handyman
  by C.L. Swinney

- Hell's Angels Biker Wars
  by RJ Parker

- The Dark Strangler
  by Michael Newton

- The Alcohol Murders
  by Harriet Fox

- Peter Woodcock: Canada's Youngest
  Serial Killer
  by Mark Bourrie

- Clifford Olson: The Beast of British Columbia
  by Elizabeth Broderick

- Taking Tori
  by Kelly Banaski

View these and future books in this collection at:

rjpp.ca/CC-CRIMES-CANADA-BOOKS

About The Author

Edward Butts was born in Toronto, but grew up in Guelph, Ontario, and has always considered it his hometown. He attended the University of Waterloo and spent eight years teaching at a school in the Dominican Republic.

Edward has written more than twenty books for both adults and juvenile readers. They include: *Simon Girty: Wilderness Warrior, Wrong Side of the Law,* and *Behind the Badge: Crime Fighters Through History.* Several of his books have been nominated for awards. Ed also wrote the lyrics for educational songs for children. As a freelance writer, Edward has contributed articles to many publications, including, the Toronto Star, the Globe & Mail and the Guelph Mercury. He lives in Guelph with his daughter and grandson.

Contact Information

Email - edpbutts@yahoo.com

Facebook -
https://www.facebook.com/ed.butts.73?fref=ts

Bibliography

Books

Anderson, Frank, W. *Old Time Western Sheriffs & Outlaws: Vol. 1*, Humboldt, SK, Gopher Books, 1999

Esslinger, Michael, *Alcatraz: A Definitive History of the Penitentiary Years*, Carmel, CA, Ocean View Publishing, 2003

Giles, Ted, *Patty Cannon: Woman of Mystery*, Easton, MD, Easton Publishing Co., 1965

Guerin, Eddie, *I Was a Bandit*, New York, Doubleday, Doran & Co., 1929

Helmer, William J. and Rick Mattix, *The Complete Public Enemy Almanac*, Nashville, TN, Cumberland House, 2007

Karpis, Alvin, and Bill Trent, *Public Enemy Number One,* Toronto, McClelland & Stewart, 1971; and Robert Livesey, *On The Rock: Twenty-five Years in Alcatraz*, Oakville, ON, Little Brick Schoolhouse Inc., 2008 (first published by Musson Book Co., Don Mills, ON, 1980)

King, Betty Nygaard, *Hell Hath No Fury: Famous Women in Crime*, Ottawa, ON, Borealis Press, 2001

O'Connor, Darcy and Miranda O'Connor, *Montreal's Irish Mafia*, Mississauga, ON, John Wiley & Sons Canada, 2011

O'Faolain, Nuala, *The Story of Chicago May*, New York, Riverhead Books, 2005

Pfeifer, Jeffrey, and Ken Leyton Brown, *Death By Rope Vol. 1: 1867-1923*, Regina, SK, Centax Books, 2007

Williams, David Ricardo, *Call In Pinkerton's*, Dundurn, Toronto, 1998

Newspapers and Periodicals

The New York *Times*

The Ottawa *Citizen*

The Toronto *Globe & Mail*

The Toronto *Star*

The Vancouver *Province*

The Welland *Tribune*

Lemay, Georges, *Je Suis Coupable*, Editions ABC, Montreal, 1952 - photos